FreeHand Graphics Studio 7 Interactive

macromedia®
PRESS

FreeHand Graphics Studio 7 Interactive
Macromedia, Inc.

Published by Macromedia Press, in association with Peachpit Press, a division of Addison Wesley Longman.

Macromedia Press
2414 Sixth Street
Berkeley, CA 94710
510/548-4393
520/548-5991 (fax)
Find us on the World Wide Web at:
http://www.peachpit.com
http://www.macromedia.com

Cover design by Supon Design Group

ISBN 0-201-68837-9

9 8 7 6 5 4 3 2 1

Printed and bound in the United States of America

Credits

Producer:
Karen Tucker, Macromedia

Authors and Instructional Designers:
Thomas Faist and Craig Faist, Datrix Media Group

Programmer and Technical Lead:
John Szymanski

Editor:
Judy Ziajka

Audio Recording:
Dubey Tunes

Voice Talent:
Mary Dilts

Artwork:
Julia Sifers, Glasgow & Associates
Thomas Faist and Craig Faist, Datrix Media Group

Production:
Rick Gordon, Emerald Valley Graphics
Myrna Vladic, Bad Dog Graphics
Debbie Roberti, Espresso Graphics

Indexer:
Steve Rath

Thanks to:
Rocky Angelucci, Marjorie Baer, Alex Bohn, Darcy DiNucci, Joel Dreskin, Tom Hale, David Mendals, Joanne Watkins, Bob Whitney

Publisher:
Tim Bigoness, Macromedia

Contents

Introduction
How to Use Macromedia Interactive

Note: This CD includes a full-featured copy of FreeHand 7 along with FreeHand's complete online help. However, you cannot save the files you create. When you load the CD, the program checks your computer to see if you have sufficient random-access memory (RAM) for the practice files to load automatically. If you don't, a screen message tells you how to load the files. If you have at least 16 megabytes of RAM, everything will probably be done automatically for you as the program runs.

Welcome to *FreeHand Graphics Studio Interactive.*

This training program shows you how to use the features of FreeHand 7 to create graphics, illustrations, and documents. It introduces the other components of FreeHand Graphics Studio (FGS)—Extreme 3D, xRes, and Fontographer—and explores the process of creating Shockwave graphics you can put on the Internet.

The CD-plus-workbook format *walks you through it* and then *lets you do it.*

First Macromedia instructors virtually operate your computer to show you exactly how each feature is used. These instructors guide you through the lessons just like an instructor in the classroom—it's the next best thing to getting the teachers in the box along with the CD!

Then *you do it!* Any time you want to practice precisely what you've seen demonstrated, you just click the Practice button. The practice lesson opens in FreeHand displaying the same elements you've seen in the animated tutorial. You can then perform the same operations and use the same techniques you've seen demonstrated in the interactive tutorial, working with the same graphic elements on the screen.

This workbook will help you duplicate the step-by-step activities the instructors show you on the CD. You can go back and forth between the audiovisual tutorials and the practice lessons.

This training program, written in Macromedia Director, is completely interactive. You choose what lessons you want to learn, and in what order, and you decide when to watch the instructors demonstrate the tasks and when to practice them on your own. Best of all, you really use FreeHand and the other FGS applications.

The instructions in this workbook assume that you're a beginner with FreeHand; the workbook starts with the basics and builds slowly from there. However, this workbook also assumes that you're familiar with the basic operations of your computer—how to choose items from menus, save files, and so on. For more information on such tasks, refer to the documentation that came with your computer.

The Read Me file on the CD provides the latest information about the program along with easy-to-follow instructions on how to get started.

Now it's time for you to begin using the FreeHand Graphics Studio.

Required Hardware and Software

You will need the following equipment to practice the lessons described in this workbook:

Windows

486/50 or faster processor, Pentium or Pentium Pro processor recommended

Windows 95, Windows NT, or later

16 megabytes (MB) or more of available RAM (24 MB recommended)

Hard disk with a minimum of 5 MB of free disk space (50 MB required to install all four FreeHand Graphics Studio applications)

CD-ROM drive, 4X (4 speed) recommended

For Section 10, you will need a browser that supports Shockwave and the Shockwave for FreeHand Plug-In to prepare graphics as Shockwave elements for use in Web pages. See Macromedia's Web site at http://www.macromedia.com for more information.

Macintosh

68040 or faster processor, Power PC processor recommended

Macintosh System 7.1 or later

16 MB or more of available RAM (24 MB recommended)

Hard disk with a minimum of 5 MB of free disk space (50 MB required to install all four FreeHand Graphics Studio applications)

CD-ROM drive, 4X (4 speed) recommended

For Section 10, you will need a browser that supports Shockwave and the Shockwave for FreeHand Plug-In to prepare graphics as Shockwave elements for use in Web pages. See Macromedia's Web site at http://www.macromedia.com for more information.

Installation

You can use *FreeHand Graphics Studio Interactive* in three ways: You can run FreeHand from the CD, from your hard disk, or from your hard disk with your own copies of the FGS applications. Your choice will be determined by the amount of space you have on your hard disk, the speed of your computer, and whether you want to use the special training version of FreeHand that comes on the *FreeHand Graphics Studio Interactive* CD.

To practice using the other three FreeHand Graphics Studio applications—Extreme 3D, xRes, and Fontographer—you must install the applications on your hard drive, either from the original disks included when you purchased the FreeHand Graphics Studio or the special training versions provided on the *FreeHand Graphics Studio Interactive* CD. When it comes time to practice a lesson in one of these applications, the tutorial and workbook will instruct you to open a specific file or application.

If you have the FreeHand Graphics Studio applications installed on your computer, you may want to use your own copy of each application. The main advantage of doing so is that you will be able to save the work you do in the lessons. With the training versions of the software, you won't be able to save your work. Note, however, that *FreeHand Graphics Studio Interactive* was designed so that you can learn the FreeHand Graphics Studio applications without saving files.

Run the Installer

No matter which of the three ways you choose to run FreeHand, you will need to run the installer.

Double-click the Installer icon on the CD to install the tutorial onto your hard drive. This automatically creates a folder named FGS7 on your hard drive.

Run the Training Version of FreeHand from Your Hard Drive (Option 1, Recommended)

If you need faster performance and do not have your own copy of FreeHand already installed on your hard drive, you can install and run the special training version of FreeHand from your hard drive.

From the CD, run the FreeHand installer to install the training version of FreeHand on your hard drive.

After you have installed the training version of FreeHand, follow the instructions below for the platform you are using.

Windows: The tutorial will use the training version of FreeHand installed on your hard drive.

Macintosh: Locate the training version of FreeHand 7 now on your hard drive. In the FGS7 folder on your hard drive, delete the alias for FreeHand. Then create a new alias for the training version of FreeHand 7 now on your hard drive. Check that the alias name is *FreeHand7*—use that *exact* name; *do not* type *FreeHand 7.0* or any other variation of the name or use any extra spaces. Be sure to put the alias in the FGS7 folder. The tutorial will then use the training version of FreeHand installed on your hard drive.

Now you are ready to run the tutorial. To run the tutorial, open the FGS7 folder icon on your hard drive and then double-click the Instruct icon. The tutorial will use the training version of FreeHand 7 now installed on your hard drive. The CD is still active in this mode. The tutorial files that you access from your hard drive will actually run from the CD, but the application will open more quickly.

Run Your Own Copy of FreeHand from the Hard Drive (Option 2)

If you want to use your own copy of FreeHand 7 and the other FGS applications so you can save your work, make sure your copy of FreeHand is installed on your hard drive and then follow the instructions for your platform.

Windows: The tutorial will use your version of FreeHand installed on your hard drive.

Macintosh: Locate your own copy of the FreeHand 7 application. In the FGS7 folder on your hard drive, delete the alias for FreeHand. Then create a new alias for the copy of FreeHand 7 on your hard drive. Check that the alias name is *FreeHand7*—use that *exact* name; *do not* type *FreeHand 7.0* or any other variation of the name or use any extra spaces. Be sure to put the alias in the FGS7 folder. The tutorial will then use your version of FreeHand installed on your hard drive.

Now you are ready to run the tutorial. To run the tutorial, open the FGS7 folder icon on your hard drive and then double-click the Instruct icon. The tutorial will use your version of FreeHand 7. The CD is still active in this mode. The tutorial files that you access from your hard disk will actually run from the CD, but the application will open more quickly, and you will be able to save your work.

Run FreeHand from the CD (Option 3)

To practice the lessons using the training version of FreeHand 7 provided on the CD, open the FGS7 folder icon on your hard drive and then double-click the Instruct icon to begin. The program will use the training version of FreeHand 7 provided on the CD.

How to Begin

When you are ready to begin the tutorial:

1 **Open the FGS7 folder icon on your hard drive.**

2 **Double-click the Instruct icon.**
You'll see the FreeHand Graphics Studio Interactive opening screen followed by the main menu, from which you'll choose your lessons.

Main Menu

The main menu lists the 10 sections of *FreeHand Graphics Studio Interactive* as well as the lessons within each section.

You can click the name of a section or lesson to go directly to that part of the program. You can also use the scroll bar at the right of the menu to scroll to any item in the list.

Notice that the mouse pointer is a white arrow when it is not over a clickable area (hot text, such as one of the section names, or a button). When the area is clickable, the pointer turns into a hand.

Changes in the color of menu items help you track your progress through this *Macromedia Interactive* tutorial. When you click a section or lesson, its name in the menu turns light green, so you know you've opened that part of the program. If in addition to opening and viewing a section you also *practice* it, the menu item turns red so you know you have tried it yourself. When you quit the tutorial, you will be asked if you want to save these settings so they will be recorded for future use. If you click the Save Settings button, the tutorial will remember which lessons you have already opened the next time you use the tutorial.

You can clear the highlighting from these entries at any time: Simply hold down the Alt key (Windows) or Option key (Macintosh) and click the word *Macromedia* below the menu. (Try this now if you have been clicking the menu to see what happens.) Any highlighted text returns to its original white color.

View Art Gallery

At the top of the menu is an instruction—CLICK HERE TO VIEW ART GALLERY—that lets you view a gallery of art created with FreeHand Graphics Studio 7. If you click this text, the CD displays a series of artwork. You can interrupt the playback by clicking the Menu button, which returns you to the main menu.

You can use the control panel (as described in later in this introduction) to stop, fast-forward, or fast-reverse. When you pause the playback, you can simply click the Play button to continue.

Play All Sections

Near the top of the menu is an instruction—CLICK HERE TO PLAY ALL SECTIONS NONSTOP—that lets you watch all the lessons on the CD continuously. If you click this text, the tutorial will play without interruption unless you stop it. You can interrupt nonstop play by clicking the Practice button, which takes you to a separate practice session, or the Menu button, which returns you to the main menu. If you interrupt continuous play in either of these ways, it won't be continued after the interruption.

You can use the control panel (as described later in this introduction) to stop, fast-forward, or fast-reverse during continuous play. When you pause a lesson in any of these ways, you can simply click the Play button to continue.

What's New

At the bottom of the menu (reached by scrolling) is the title What's New at Macromedia Press. You can click this text for additional Macromedia Press information.

Section Interface

If you decide not to play through the disk nonstop, you can choose each lesson separately, as described here.

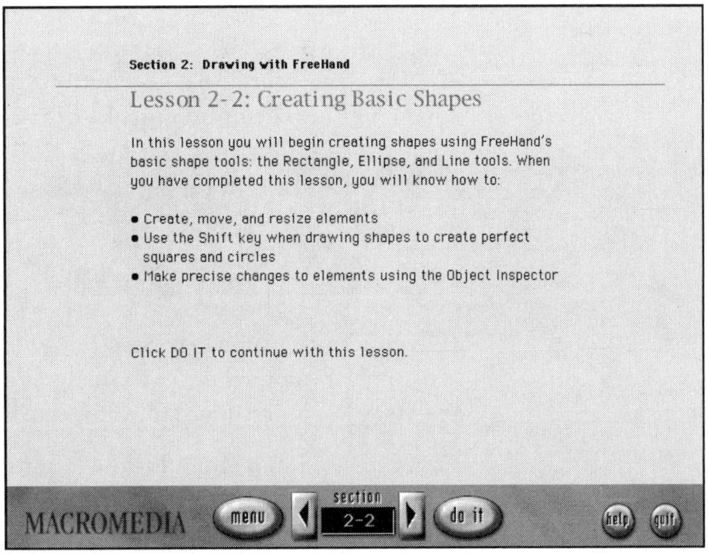

Practice opening a lesson by clicking the following line in the menu:

2-2 Creating Basic Shapes

The first screen you see describes what you will learn in that lesson. It also gives you a chance to change your mind about playing the lesson.

At the bottom of the screen is the control bar, which is available on every screen of the tutorial. You'll use it to control the operation of the tutorial.

The control bar gives you several navigational choices. You can use the arrow buttons to navigate through the lessons in a section. If you decide you don't want to stay in this lesson or section, you can click Menu to return to the main menu to make a different selection. Click Do It to begin the tutorial for this lesson.

For now, click Do It. When the movie starts to play, the Do It button changes to the Practice button, and a control panel appears at the lower left of the control bar.

Control Panel

The control panel gives you complete control over the presentation. For instance, if you want to stop the tutorial briefly while you study a particular part of the interface, you can click the Stop button (which then turns into a Play button). To start again, you click the same button. The button toggles between Stop and Play.

On either side of the Play/Stop button are Fast Reverse and Fast Forward. If you hold down the mouse on these buttons, the program will play fast in the direction you selected until you release the mouse.

You can also jump around within a tutorial by clicking the progress bar. This indicator—a series of 10 lights—shows approximately where you are in the tutorial. You can click any of these lights to rapidly change your location in the lesson.

You can adjust the sound volume with the arrows next to the speaker icon. To increase the volume, you hold down the mouse on the up arrow; to lower the volume, you hold down the mouse on the down arrow.

Section Indicator

You can't get lost in the tutorials because the section indicator always shows where you are. The number of the current section and lesson is automatically displayed here when you make a selection from the menu, and that number remains displayed until you select a different lesson.

On each side of the section indicator are arrow buttons pointing left and right. You can click these arrow buttons to move from the lesson you are in to the opening text screen of either the preceding or the following lesson within the current section. The indicator number changes as you change lessons.

Although you can click the arrows to browse within a section, you can't stray outside of the current section. To move to a lesson in another section, you need to return to the main menu using the Menu button.

You can use the arrow buttons any time they appear—whether or not a movie is playing. Try the arrow buttons now, but be sure to note where you are so you can return to the current lesson.

You can start the movie in any lesson you are browsing by clicking Do It.

How to Practice

An important feature of this tutorial is the capability to practice the lessons. You can click the Practice button while a movie is playing or after you have viewed it to the end.

The practice feature enables you to leave the tutorial, open the actual application, and work with a file that has the same elements that the tutorial uses. This workbook will guide you through the lesson; it contains step-by-step instructions that match the steps the instructors teach on the CD.

If your computer has sufficient RAM, the program will automatically launch FreeHand and open the practice files, and when you leave the practice session, it will return you to the tutorials. If this doesn't happen automatically, you can open the practice files yourself.

When practicing a lesson in Extreme 3D, xRes, or Fontographer, you will be instructed which practice file to open yourself.

Note: All of the practice lessons are in a folder called Lessons on the CD. You double-click the relevant file to open it. Then follow the step-by-step directions in this workbook to complete the work in the file. When you're finished, quit FreeHand and return to the tutorials by clicking the Instruct icon, just as you did when you first launched the program.

Click the Practice button in Section 2-2 now.

The first practice screen explains that you're about to start a practice routine for the lesson you've been watching. You should read this screen and then click Practice again to continue. At this point you'll either see the practice file start to open, or you'll see a message explaining how to open the file yourself. Then turn to the corresponding lesson in this workbook and follow the steps. When you're through practicing, choose File > Exit (Windows) or File > Quit (Macintosh) to return to the main menu.

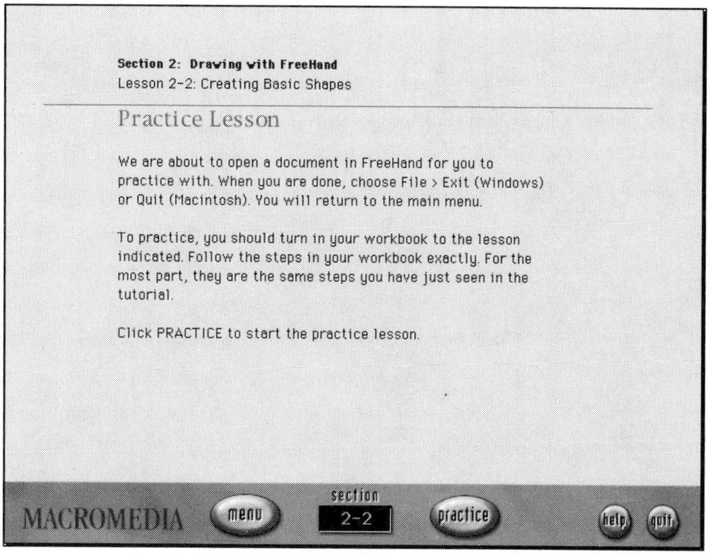

The practice files you'll use are numbered the same as the corresponding tutorial lessons: 1-1, 1-2, and so on. The corresponding workbook lessons are also numbered the same as the tutorials.

Online help is available at any time. Simply click the Help button, and a help screen will appear to show you all available options at that point in the program.

When you're ready to leave the program, click the Quit button. (When you're in a practice lesson, you quit by choosing File > Exit (Windows) or File > Quit (Macintosh). And now, you're ready to start.

One last note: FreeHand will remember which panels you opened in previous lessons, and those panels will remain open through subsequent work sessions. This is very often convenient, but it means that you may have panels open that differ from those shown in this workbook and CD—so if you're instructed to open a panel that's already open, that's why. In fact, you should feel free to take charge of your working environment as you progress through this tutorial. If you would like to open, move, or resize a panel for your own convenience, don't hesitate to do so.

1 Getting Started with FreeHand

This section consists of three lessons:

- FreeHand Basics
- Organizing Your Workspace
- Getting Help

FreeHand's drawing and layout tools can be used to develop everything from the simplest illustrations to the most complex designs. The extensive controls FreeHand gives you over graphics, colors, type, and imported artwork make it a powerhouse for any graphic design project.

This section introduces you to FreeHand's most important windows and controls, helps you organize your working environment, and shows you how to find answers quickly using FreeHand's online help feature.

Lesson 1-1

FreeHand Basics

This first lesson explores the controls you use to create and modify artwork in FreeHand. You'll start with a document containing a single empty page, just as when you create a new document by choosing New from the File menu.

1 **If the practice lesson 1-1 isn't open, go to the Lessons folder on the CD and open the file named 1-1.fh7.**
A new **document window** appears displaying one page. This page is on the **pasteboard**, which is a work surface for your document. The pasteboard is 222 feet square. A FreeHand document can contain as many pages as will fit on the pasteboard, and everything on the pasteboard will be saved in the document.

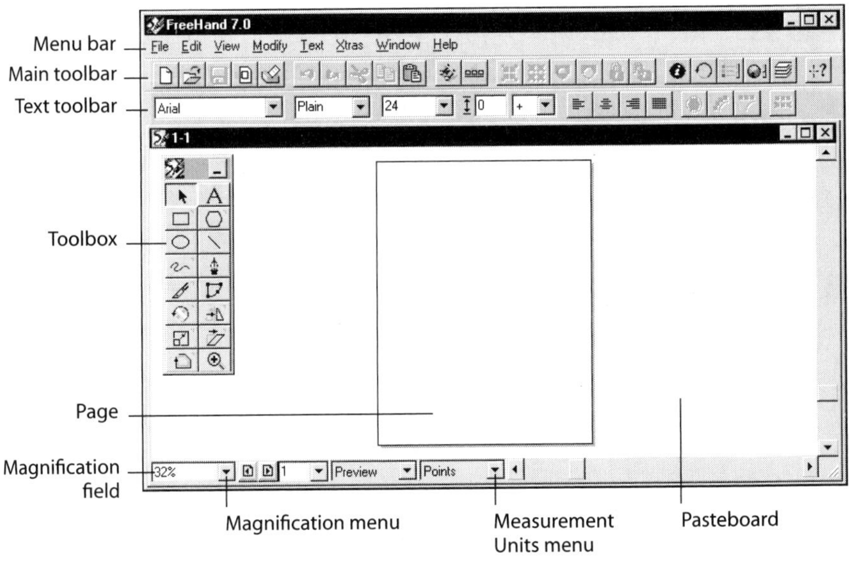

At the top of the screen, just below the menu bar, are two toolbars. The **main toolbar** gives you access to FreeHand's most frequently used features with the click of a button. The **text toolbar** contains the most common text formatting controls.

The **toolbox** appears at the left side of the screen; it contains tools you will use to create and manipulate the elements in your document. You select tools in the toolbox by clicking the mouse on the desired tool.

2 **Point to a button on the toolbar and hold the cursor still for a moment to display the name of that button.**
These **Tooltips** make it easy to identify which button to use for any specific task.

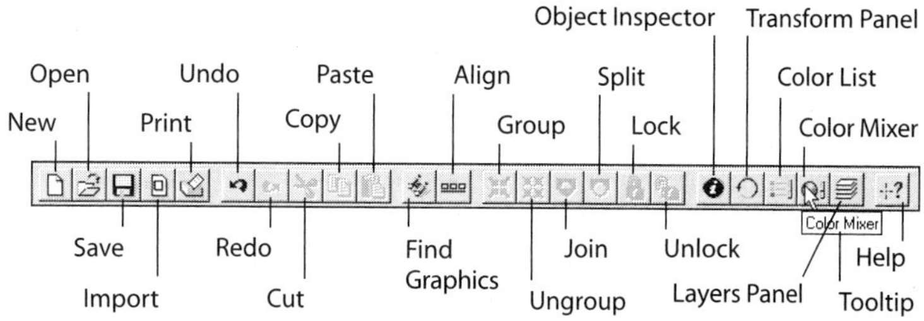

Other controls you will use frequently are located in floating **panels**, which you can display by selecting them from the Window menu.

3 **Choose Window > Panels > Color Mixer.**
This displays the Color Mixer, where you can create colors and apply them to elements in your document.

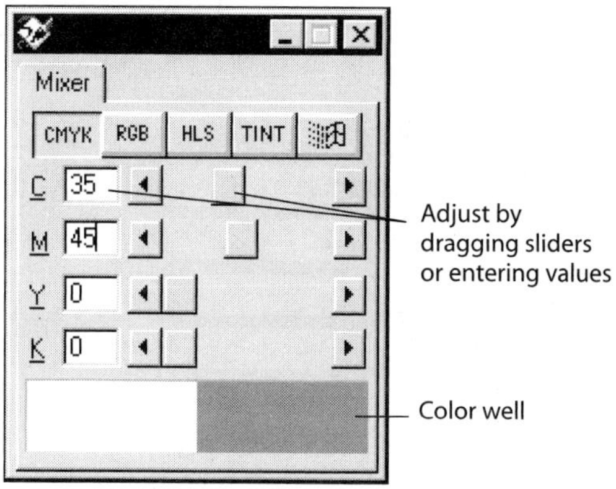

4 **Display another panel by clicking the Color List button on the toolbar or by choosing Window > Panels > Color List.**

You can add colors to the Color List so you can easily reuse in them in your document, without having to remix them in the Color Mixer.

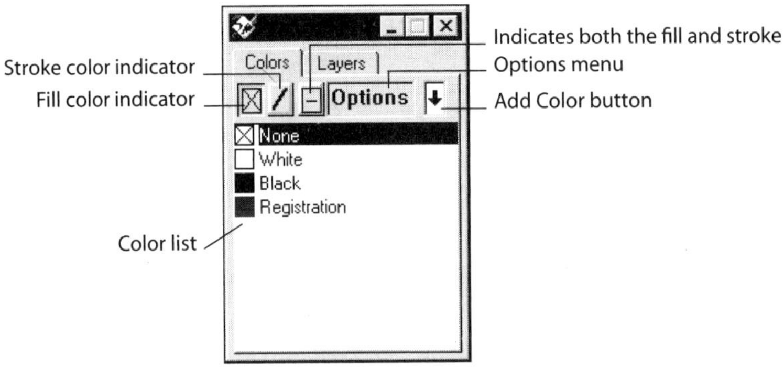

5 **Close the Color List and Color Mixer by clicking their buttons on the toolbar.**

You can leave these panels open as you work, or use the toolbar buttons to display and hide panels as needed.

6 **Now choose Window > Inspectors > Object to display the Object Inspector.**

Many of the most important controls in FreeHand have been gathered into a series of panels called Inspectors. The Object Inspector displays information about an item you select. Right now, this panel appears empty because no item is selected.

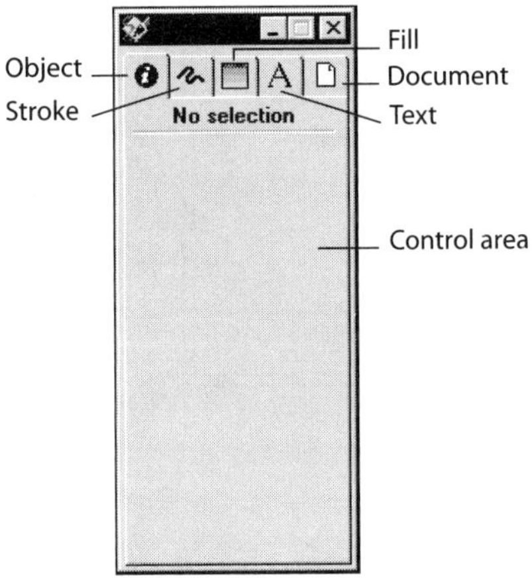

FreeHand's five Inspectors are gathered together in a **panel group**. When you display one Inspector, the others are available by clicking the **tabs** that appear across the top of the Inspector panel. The five Inspectors are the Object Inspector, Stroke Inspector, Fill Inspector, Text Inspector, and Document Inspector.

7 **Click the Document Inspector tab at the top of the Object Inspector.**

The Document Inspector appears, displaying information about the size and number of pages in your document.

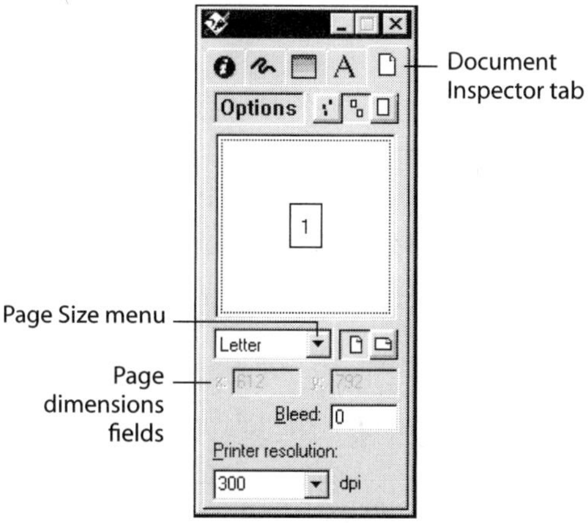

Almost every drawing task in FreeHand involves one or more of these Inspectors.

8 **Select Inches from the Measurement Units menu at the bottom edge of the document window.**

This changes the measurement units for this document. Notice that the page dimensions in the Document Inspector are now displayed in inches.

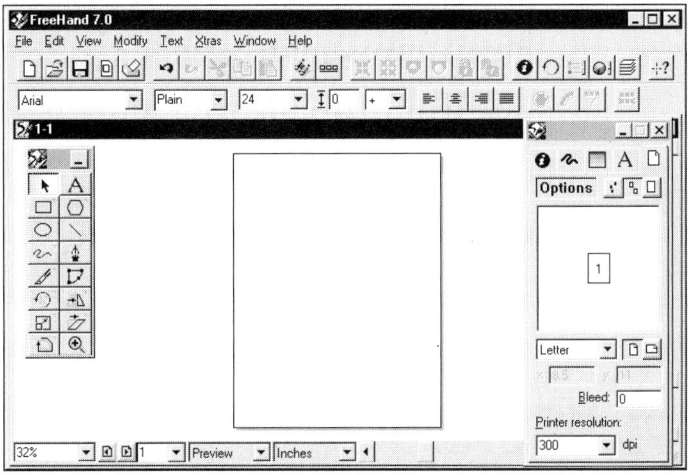

9 **Change your view of the page by choosing 25% from the Magnification menu at the lower-left edge of the document window.**

The smaller the magnification value, the more of the page you will see, though the size of the page will be reduced. A larger value lets you zoom in for a close look at details.

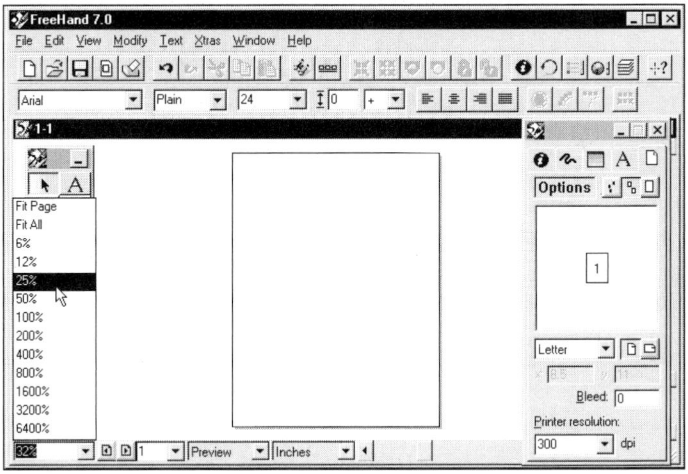

10 Change the view again, this time by typing *15* into the Magnification field and pressing Enter (Windows) or Return (Macintosh).

11 Change the view once more by choosing View > Fit To Page.

FreeHand offers several ways to complete tasks so you can use the technique that is best for you.

12 Close the Document Inspector now by clicking the close button in the panel's header bar.

Because FreeHand lets you display or hide panels at will, you always have at hand just the controls you need when creating your illustrations, designs, and layouts. You will learn more about how to use each of these elements in later sections.

You have completed this lesson and are ready to return to the tutorial.

13 Choose File > Exit (Windows) or File > Quit (Macintosh).

If you opened this lesson file from within the interactive tutorial, you will be returned to the tutorial automatically. Otherwise, you can return to the tutorial by double-clicking the Instruct icon on the CD.

Lesson 1-2

Organizing Your Workspace

FreeHand offers several ways for you to customize the organization of the panels in your workspace.

1 **If the practice lesson 1-2 isn't open, go to the Lessons folder on the CD and open the file named 1-2.fh7.**
Alternatively, you can choose File > New to display an empty page.

2 **Display the Color List by clicking its button on the toolbar or by choosing Window > Panels > Color List.**
Notice the two tabs at the top of this panel: Colors and Layers. These tabs indicate that the Color List is currently grouped with the Layers panel.

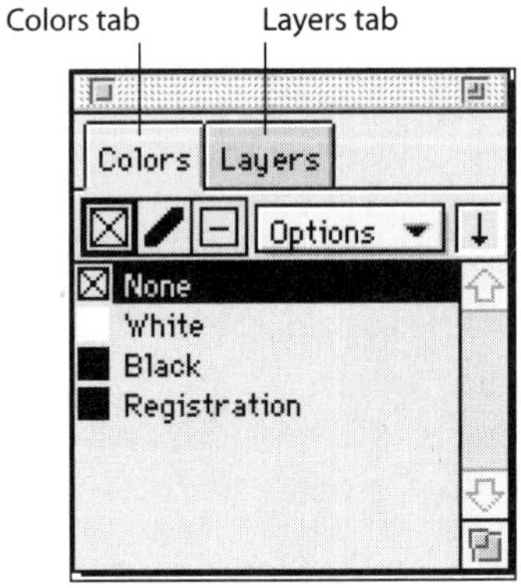

3 **Click the Layers tab to bring the Layers panel to the front of the group.**
In Section 5 you will see how to use the Layers panel to organize the artwork in your documents.

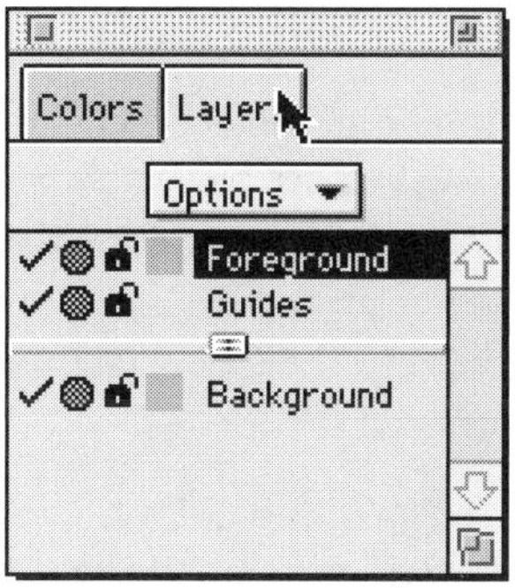

4 **Drag the Layers tab out of the panel group and release the mouse.**
This ungroups the panels so you can access both of them at the same time. Grouping panels together is just as simple.

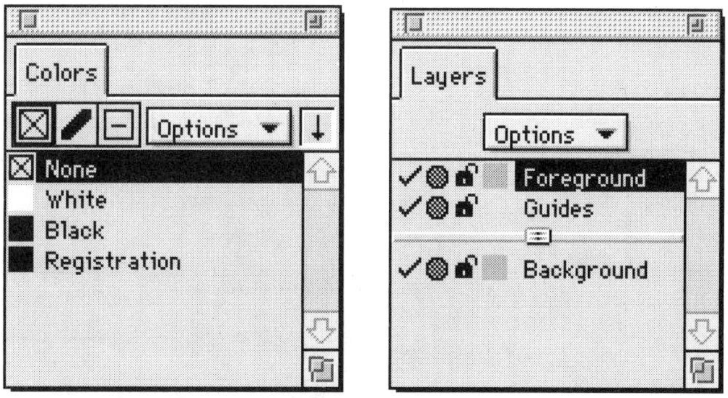

5 **Drag the Layers tab onto the Color List and release the mouse.**
The two panels are grouped together again.

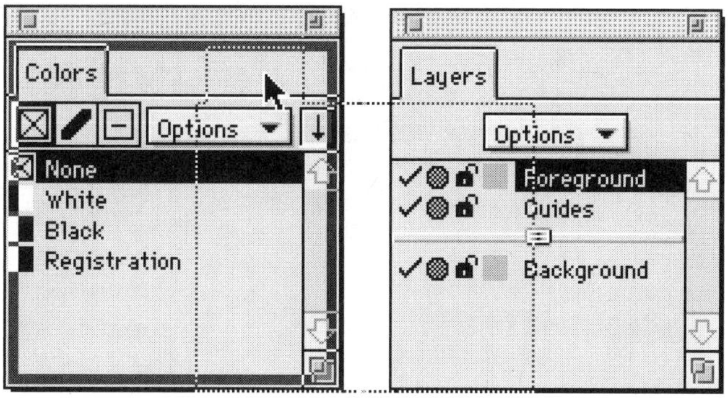

6 **Click the Colors tab to display the Color List again.**

7 **Display the Color Mixer by clicking its button on the toolbar or by choosing Window > Panels > Color Mixer.**
You will often use the Color Mixer and Color List panels at the same time, creating new colors in the Color Mixer and then adding them to the Color List to make them easy to access when you need them.

8 **Move an edge of the Color Mixer toward an edge of the Color List by dragging the header bar at the top of the panel.**
When the edges of the panels are within 12 pixels of one another, they will snap together. The panels are aligned, but they remain independent of one another—you can move or resize one without affecting the other.

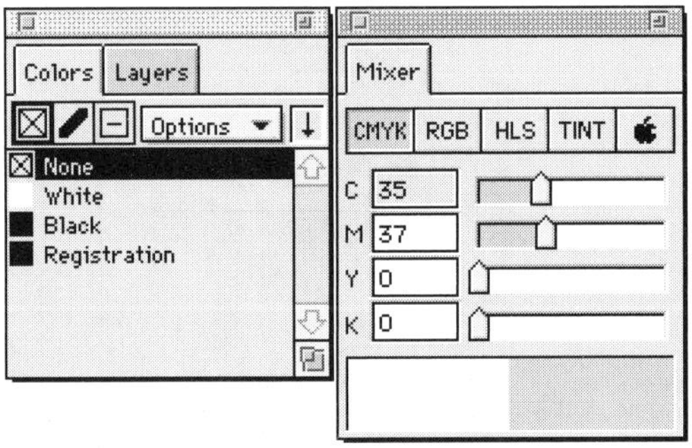

9 **Collapse the Color List by clicking the minimize button (in Windows) or zoom box (on the Macintosh) in its header bar.**
The Color List collapses without affecting the Color Mixer. You can collapse panels when you want to hide controls temporarily while keeping them readily available.

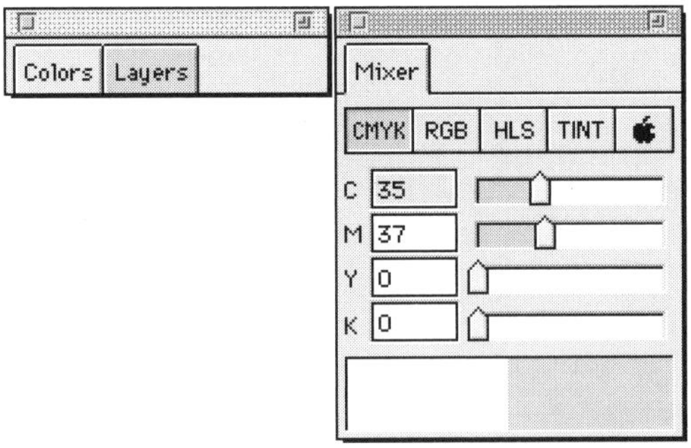

10 Expand the Color List to see the entire panel again and then move the Color Mixer away from the Color List.

In addition to grouping panels together and aligning them with one another, you can connect the edges of panels so the panels behave as if they were one.

11 Drag one panel toward the edge of the other while pressing the Control key on the keyboard. Release the mouse when the two panels snap together.

This **docks** the panels. Notice the **panel dock** that appears in the space between the panels.

Panel dock

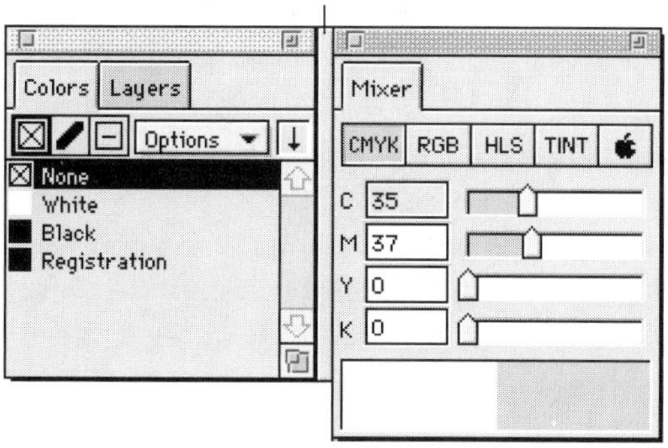

Docking can make it easier for you to work with several panels at once. Unlike the panels in a panel group, docked panels are visible at the same time.

12 Move the Color List by dragging its header bar.

Docked panels move together.

13 Collapse and then expand one of the panels.

When panels are docked, they collapse and expand together.

14 Undock the panels by clicking the panel dock between the two panels.

The panel dock disappears, and the two panels are independent once again.

As you work with FreeHand, you can position, group, dock, and collapse panels as needed. Remember that you can also show and hide panels using the buttons on the toolbar or the commands in the Window menu.

You have completed this lesson and are ready to return to the tutorial.

13 Choose File > Exit (Windows) or File > Quit (Macintosh).
If you opened this lesson file from within the interactive tutorial, you will be returned to the tutorial automatically. Otherwise, you can return to the tutorial by double-clicking the Instruct icon on the CD.

Lesson 1-3

Getting Help

FreeHand offers an online help system you can turn to if you have questions as you work.

1 **If the practice lesson 1-3 isn't open, go to the Lessons folder on the CD and open the file named 1-3.fh7.**
   Alternatively, you can choose File > New to display an empty page.

2 **Windows: Click the Help button on the right side of the toolbar.**
   A new window appears displaying the Help Contents screen

   You can also display the Help window by choosing an option from the Help menu.

3 **Macintosh: Choose Help from the Apple menu.**
   A new window appears displaying the Help Contents screen.

   For more direct access to help on the Macintosh, click the Help button on the right side of the toolbar. This displays a Help cursor (which looks like a question mark). Then select a menu item or click an open panel to display help information for that item. For example, if you click the Color Mixer with the Help cursor, the Help window will open displaying information about the Color Mixer.

4 **Resize the window as needed to see the entire Contents screen.**

5 **Click a topic in the contents list, such as Using Help. Scroll down through this page of information using the scroll bars.**
A new screen containing information on that topic will appear. All green text in the help screens are hot links.

Hot link text

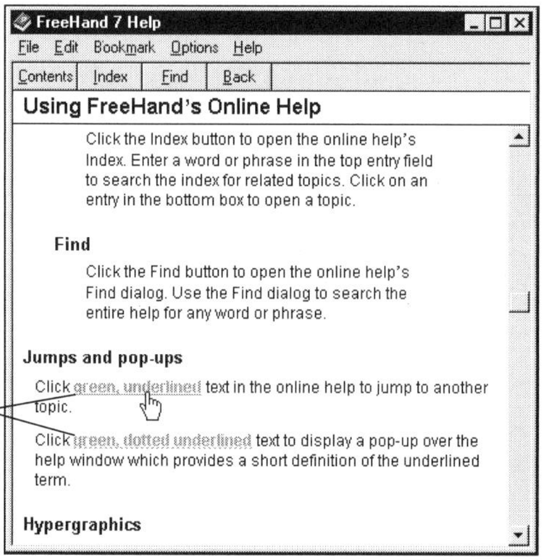

6 **Click any of the green hot link text to display additional information on the topic.**
The help system also offers other ways to locate information.

7 **Click the Index button at the top of the help screen.**
This enables you to search for a topic by name.

8 **Enter a topic, such as *color*, in the Search field at the top of this window. You can also select an item from the list of topics organized by category below. Once the desired topic is selected, click the Display button.**

Note that the list of topics changes when you enter text in the Search field so that the list displays topics that match or nearly match the text you typed.

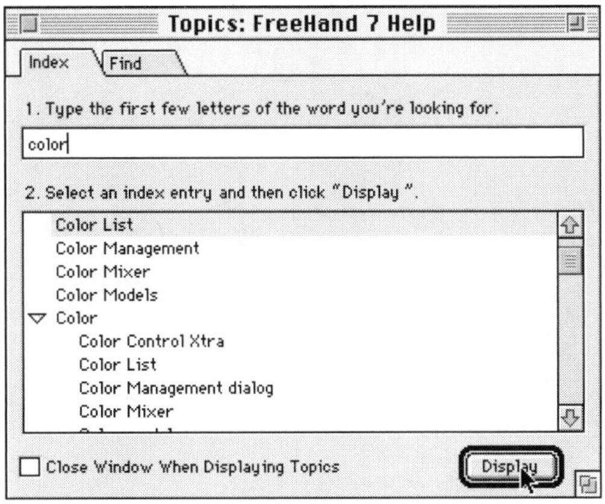

A page containing information about the selected topic appears in the Help window.

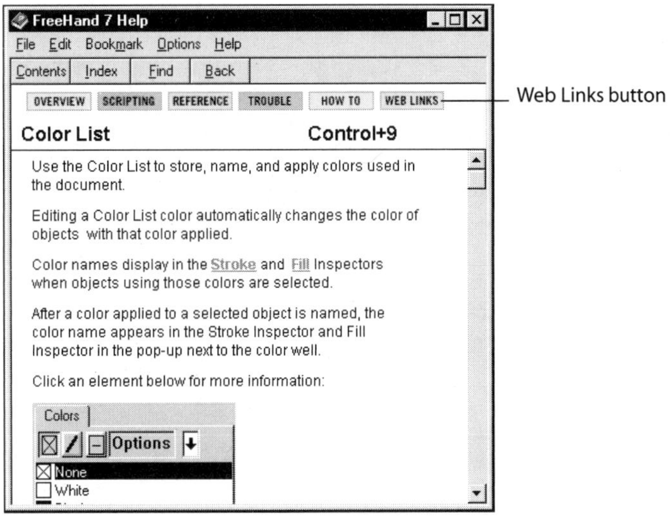

9 **Click the Web Links button at the top of the page.**

Many pages have hot link buttons across the top so you can jump directly to other topics.

As you can see, online help provides many ways for you to find the information you need.

10 **Windows: To return to FreeHand, close the Help window.**

11 **Macintosh: Choose File > Quit to quit Help and return to FreeHand.**
You have completed this lesson and are ready to return to the tutorial.

12 **Choose File > Exit (Windows) or File > Quit (Macintosh).**
If you opened this lesson file from within the interactive tutorial, you will be returned to the tutorial automatically. Otherwise, you can return to the tutorial by double-clicking the Instruct icon on the CD.

2 Drawing with FreeHand

This section consists of five lessons:

- Setting Up a Page
- Creating Basic Shapes
- Changing the Way Elements Look
- Working with Groups of Elements
- Using the Transformation Tools

This section explores concepts you will use in every FreeHand project. You will construct a simple robot illustration, and as you work you will see how to use the tools and controls introduced in the previous section to create and modify shapes on your page, and how to apply color to these elements. You will also learn how to set up a custom page size, move separate elements together as a group, and use the Transformation tools to complete the illustration.

FreeHand is an **object-oriented** drawing program. Object oriented means that your document is created from graphic objects, or shapes, rather than from individual pixels as with a **bitmap** drawing tool. Object-oriented graphics (also known as **vector** graphics) enable you to scale FreeHand artwork to any size or output resolution with no loss of quality.

Lesson 2-1

Setting Up a Page

In any FreeHand document, you can specify a custom page size. You'll see how to do that here.

1 **If the practice lesson 2-1 isn't open, go to the Lessons folder on the CD and open the file named 2-1.fh7.**
This document contains one empty letter-size page.

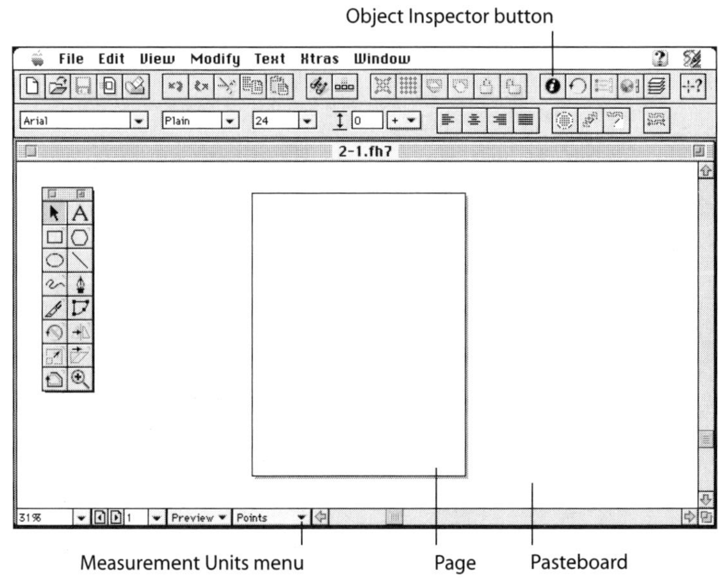

2 **Display the Object Inspector by clicking its button on the toolbar or by choosing Window > Inspectors > Object.**
The five Inspectors are grouped together, with a tab for each one displayed across the top of the panel.

3 **Click the Document Inspector tab at the top right of the panel.**
The Document Inspector appears, displaying the controls that allow you to specify a page size and orientation.

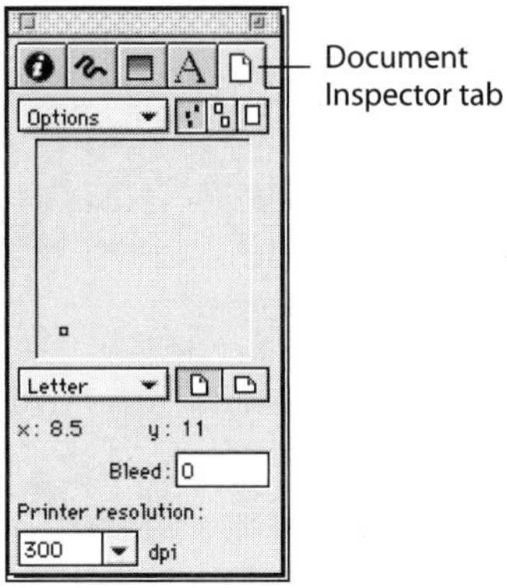

4 **Choose inches from the Measurement Units menu at the bottom of the document window**
This changes the measurement units for this document to inches. Now you will specify a custom page size.

5 **Change the Page Size menu in the Document Inspector from Letter to Custom. Then change the dimensions of the page to 4 by 7 inches and press Enter (Windows) or Return (Macintosh).**

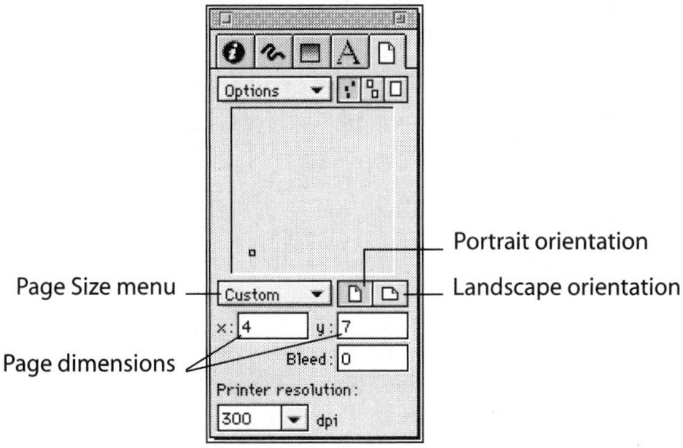

The page is automatically updated to the new dimensions. The Document Inspector also provides buttons for changing the page from Portrait (vertical) to Landscape (horizontal) orientation, if needed. For this project, you will leave the page set to Portrait orientation.

6 **Choose View > Page Rulers to display rulers along the left and top edges of the document window. Then choose View > Fit To Page.**
Fit To Page adjusts your view so the entire page fills the document window.

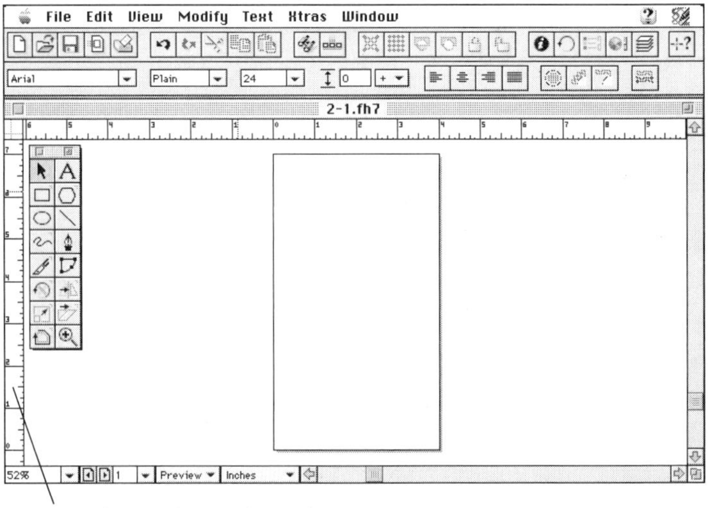

Point here to drag a ruler guide

7 **Point to the middle of the ruler at the left side of the document window and drag a ruler guide out onto the page. Position it approximately 2 inches from the left edge of the page and release the mouse button.**
These nonprinting guides will help you position elements on your page. They can be added to your page by dragging from either ruler. FreeHand also offers a more precise way to add guides to your page.

8 **Choose View > Guides > Edit to display the Guides dialog box.**
In this dialog box you can see the position of the ruler guide that you just added to the page. It may not be positioned precisely at 2 inches, but that is easy to correct.

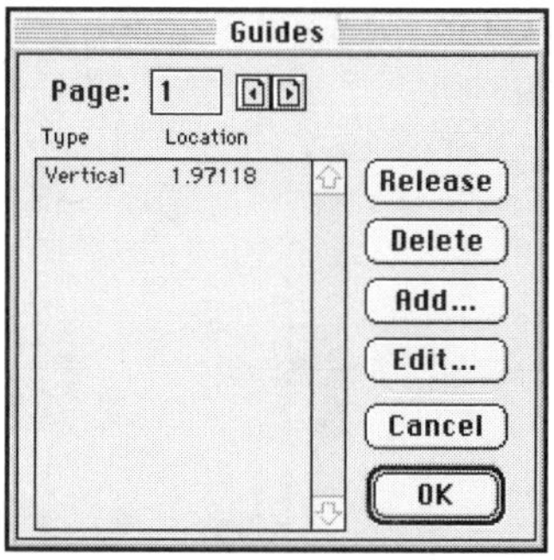

9 **If the location of the guide you just added to the list is not 2 inches, click the guide in the list to select it and then click the Edit button. Change the value to 2 and click OK.**

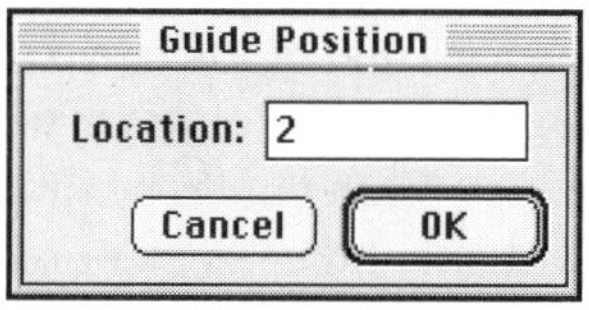

Now the ruler guide will be positioned precisely in the center of your 4-inch-wide page. Next you will some guides to help you position your work between the top and bottom of the page.

10 **Click the Add button. In the Add Guides dialog box, add three horizontal guides. Change the first position to 1 inch and the last position to 6 inches and then click Add.**

Your page is 7 inches tall, so the first and last positions you entered will position these guides 1 inch from the top and bottom of the page.

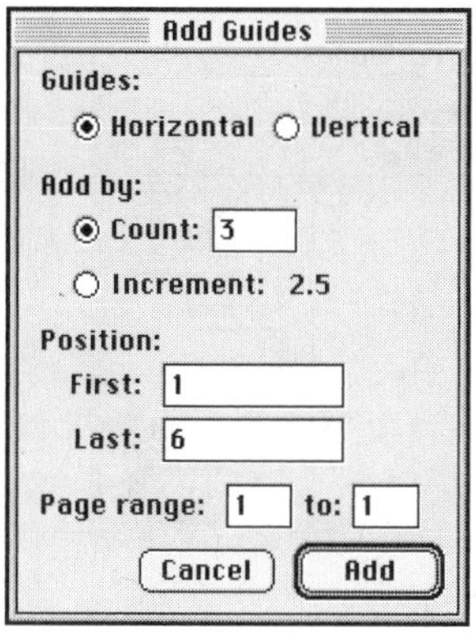

11 **Click OK in the Guides dialog box to see these new guides on your page.**

12 **Move the top ruler guide to a different position on the page by dragging it with the Pointer tool.**

You can reposition guides by dragging with the Pointer tool, just as with any other element on your page.

13 **Drag the top ruler guide off of the page and release the mouse button.**

This removes the ruler guide from the page. (Guides appear on your pages in FreeHand; the pasteboard does not display guides.) You can also use the Guides dialog box to remove guides.

14 **Choose View > Guides > Edit to display the Guides dialog box again. Select the first horizontal guide in the list and then hold down Shift and click the second horizontal guide to select both guides at the same time. Then click the Remove (Windows) or Delete (Macintosh) button.**

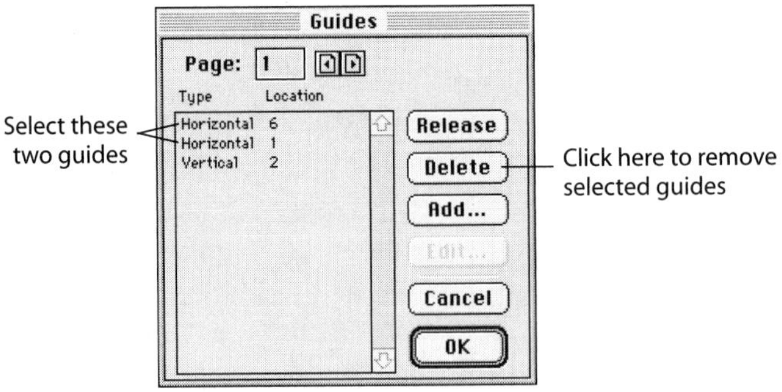

When you select one item and then hold down Shift and click another item, you add the second item to the selection. This is one way to select several items at once.

15 Click OK to close the Guides dialog box and return to the page.
Now your page is ready for you to begin constructing your artwork.

You have completed this lesson and are ready to return to the tutorial.

16 Choose File > Exit (Windows) or File > Quit (Macintosh).
If you opened this lesson file from within the interactive tutorial, you will be returned to the tutorial automatically. Otherwise, you can return to the tutorial by double-clicking the Instruct icon on the CD.

Lesson 2-2

Creating Basic Shapes

In this lesson, you will begin developing a small robot figure by creating elements with FreeHand's basic shape tools: the Rectangle, Ellipse, and Line tools.

1 **If the practice lesson 2-2 isn't open, go to the Lessons folder on the CD and open the file named 2-2.fh7.**
This document contains one 4-by-7-inch page with a vertical ruler guide positioned in the center of the page.

2 **Choose View > Magnification > 100%.**
This zooms you in so you will be able to see the artwork you'll create at actual size.

3 **Select the Rectangle tool by clicking it in the toolbox.**

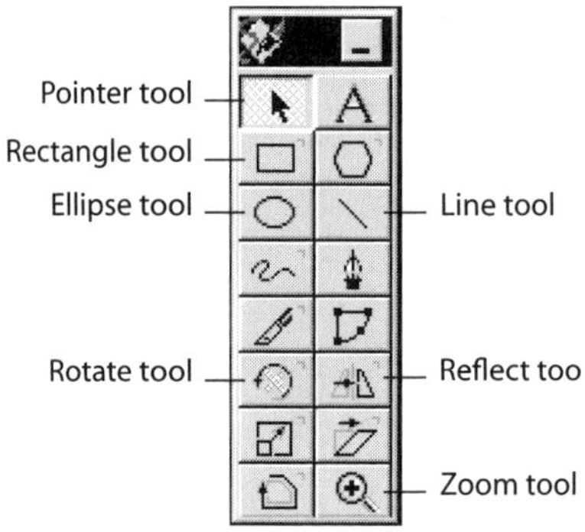

4 **Position the cursor where you want the upper-left corner of the rectangle; choose a spot near the center of the screen. Then hold down the mouse button and drag diagonally downward and to the right to create a vertical rectangle. Release the mouse when you are satisfied with the size of the rectangle.**
This rectangle will become the body of your robot. When you release the mouse, you will see four **selection boxes**, one at each corner of the rectangle, indicating that the rectangle is selected.

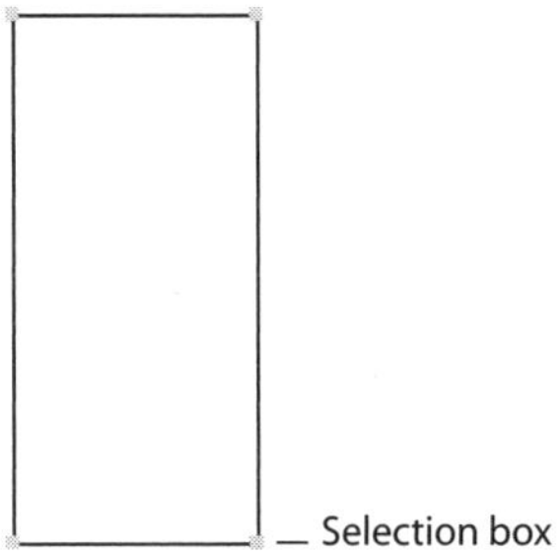

5 **Click the Pointer tool in the toolbox to choose that tool. Then point to one of the sides of the rectangle and drag to move it to a different part of the page.**

You will use the Pointer tool to work with existing elements on your page.

6 **To resize the rectangle, point to one of the selection boxes and drag.**

Dragging a selection box allows you to change the size of the selected object. FreeHand also enables you to specify a precise size for a selected element.

7 **Click the Object Inspector button on the toolbar or choose Window > Inspectors > Object.**

The Object Inspector displays information about the element that is currently selected.

8 **In the Object Inspector, select the current width of the element and enter *.5* (half an inch). Then press Tab to select the Height field and enter *1.5*.**

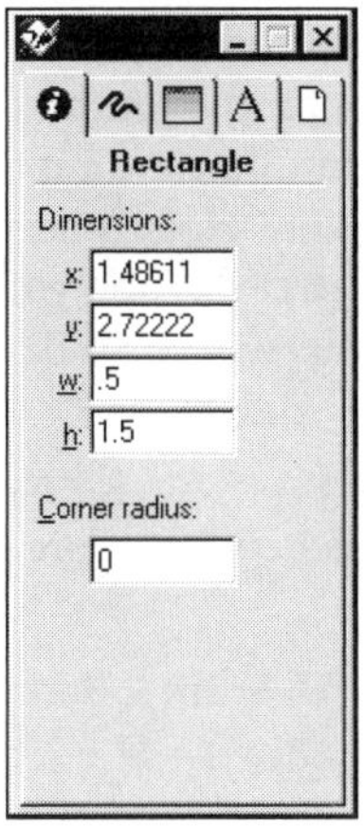

9 Press Enter (Windows) or Return (Macintosh).

The rectangle is immediately changed to the size you specified.

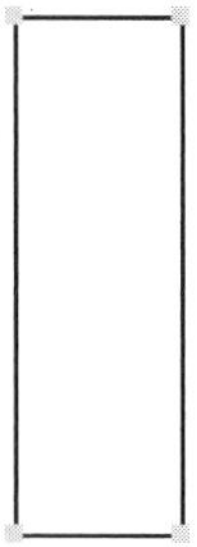

10 Draw a new rectangle just above the top of the body rectangle to create the robot's shoulders. Then draw another just below the bottom of the body to create the hips.

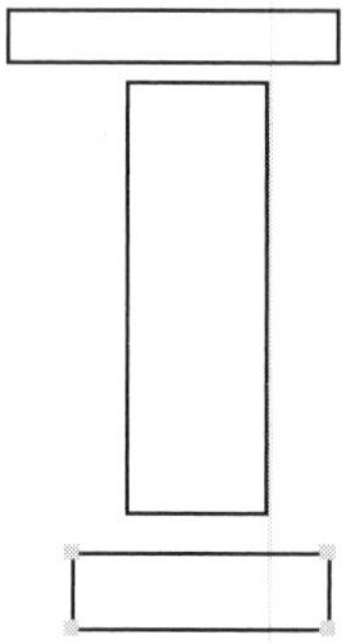

The next element you will add is a circle for the head, which you will draw with the Ellipse tool.

11 Choose the Ellipse tool from the toolbox. Position the cursor above the top rectangle on the page. Draw an ellipse just as you would a rectangle, holding down the mouse button and dragging diagonally. Hold down Shift as you draw to make this ellipse a perfect circle. When your circle is finished, release the mouse before you release Shift.

Holding Shift constrains ellipses to circles and rectangles to squares. You can see in the Object Inspector that the width and height of this new circle are identical.

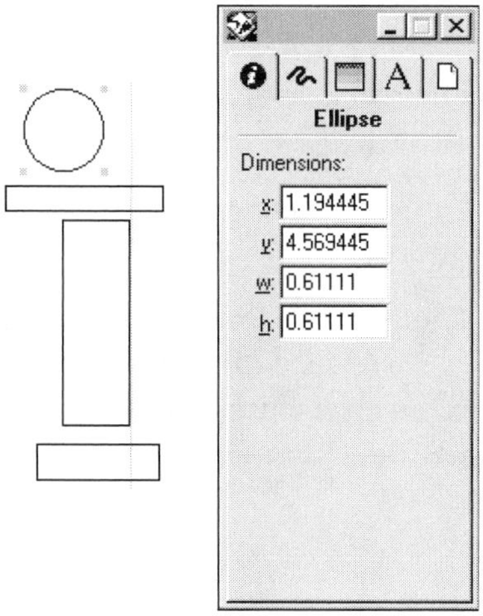

Now give your robot a spine.

12 **Choose the Line tool from the toolbox. Position the cursor above the top rectangle. Then hold down Shift and drag straight down until the line extends into the hips. Release the mouse before releasing Shift.**

Shift also constrains lines to horizontal, vertical, or 45-degree angles.

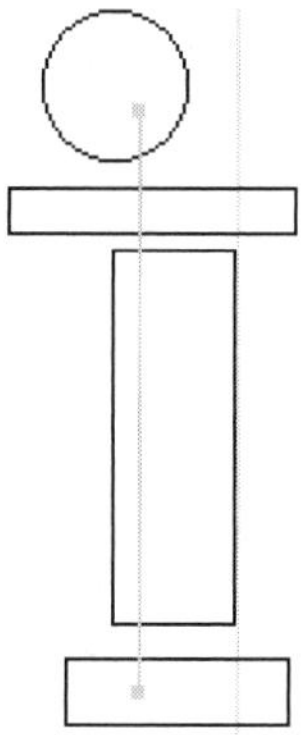

You have now created the robot's head and torso using just a few of FreeHand's basic shapes.

Note: Saving your work is an important part of creating your own projects with FreeHand Graphics Studio applications. In these lessons, you will not be reminded to save your work, since you may be using the training versions of FreeHand and the other applications supplied on this CD, which do not allow you to save.

FreeHand Graphics Studio Interactive is designed so that you can learn the FreeHand Graphics Studio applications without saving files. If you are using your own copies of the software, however, save as often as you like.

13 Close the Object Inspector by clicking the close button in its header bar.

Remember as you work to save your document frequently, just as when working with most other applications.

You have completed this lesson and are ready to return to the tutorial.

14 Choose File > Exit (Windows) or File > Quit (Macintosh).

If you opened this lesson file from within the interactive tutorial, you will be returned to the tutorial automatically. Otherwise, you can return to the tutorial by double-clicking the Instruct icon on the CD.

Lesson 2-3

Changing the Way Elements Look

Now you are ready to add some color to your robot elements.

1 **If the practice lesson 2-3 isn't open, go to the Lessons folder on the CD and open the file named 2-3.fh7.**
  This document contains five basic shapes for your robot, like the ones you created in Lesson 2-2.

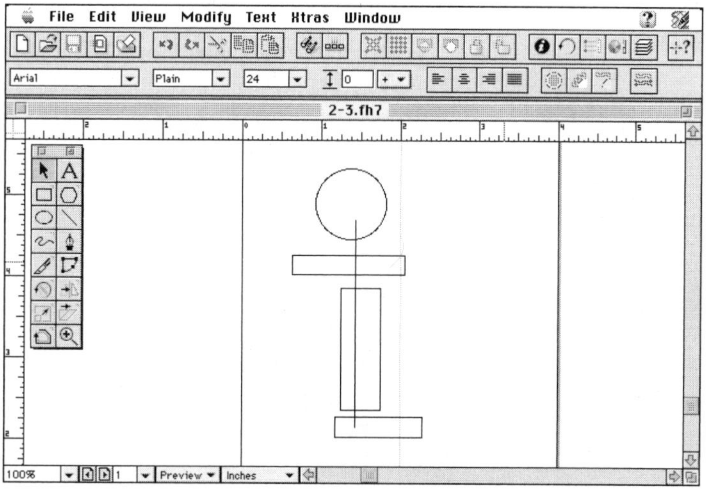

2 **Display the Color Mixer by clicking its button on the toolbar or choosing Window > Panels > Color Mixer.**
  You use the Color Mixer to create colors for use in your documents.

3 **Mix a new color by dragging the magenta and yellow sliders in the Color Mixer all the way to the right. Leave cyan and black set to zero.**

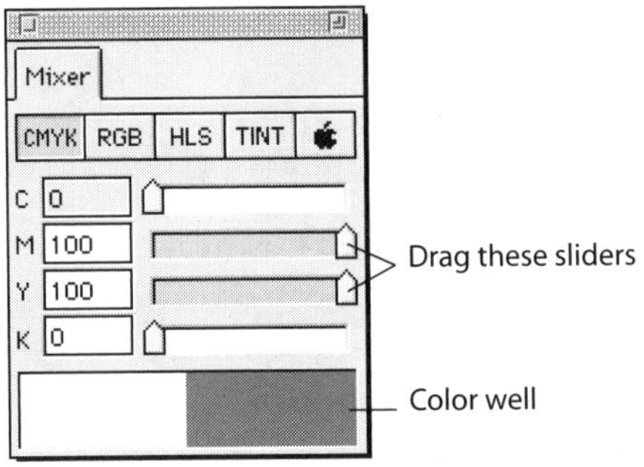

This creates a bright red. The new color appears in the color well at the bottom of the Color Mixer. So you can easily use this color again in the future, you will add it to the Color List.

4 **Display the Color List by clicking its button on the toolbar or by choosing Window > Panels > Color List.**

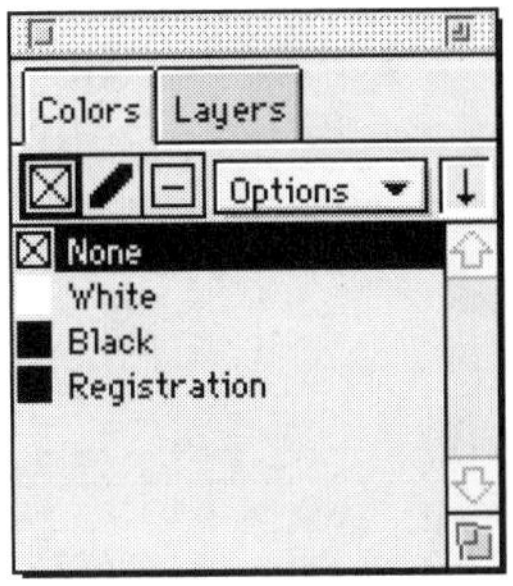

You can add colors to this panel so they can be easily accessed at any time.

5 **Drag a swatch of the red from the color well at the bottom of the Color Mixer and drop it on an empty portion of the Color List.** This adds your bright red to the list, so you can easily apply it to elements in this document.

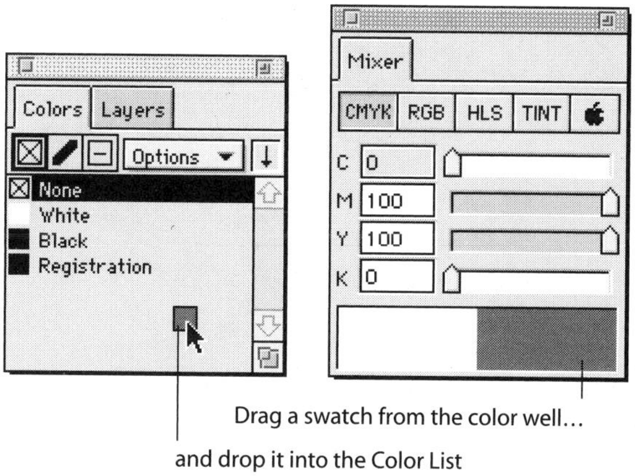

6 Drag the red swatch from the Color List and drop it inside the body rectangle on the page.

This fills the body rectangle with a solid red **fill**.

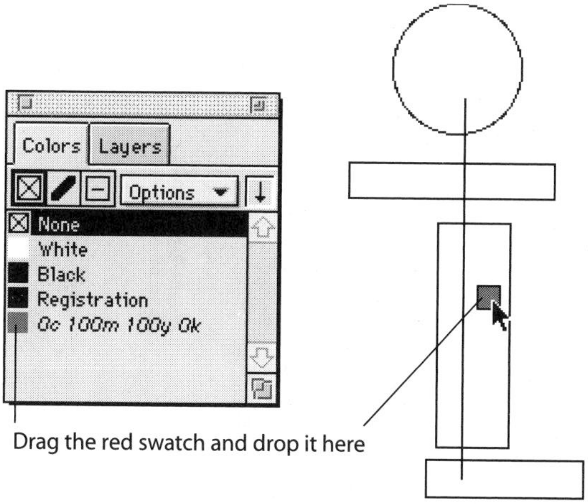

7 Fill the horizontal rectangle at the bottom of the robot body with the same red color.

If the color of the line changes instead of the fill, you must have accidentally dropped the color swatch on the line. Simply choose Undo from the Edit menu or toolbar to return the line to its original color. Then try again to drop the color swatch inside the rectangle.

8 **Create another new color in the Color Mixer. Enter *50* in the field for cyan, *50* for magenta, and *0* for yellow and black.** This creates a light blue color. This time you typed the color values instead of using the slider.

9 **Add this new color to the Color List.**

The new color appears here

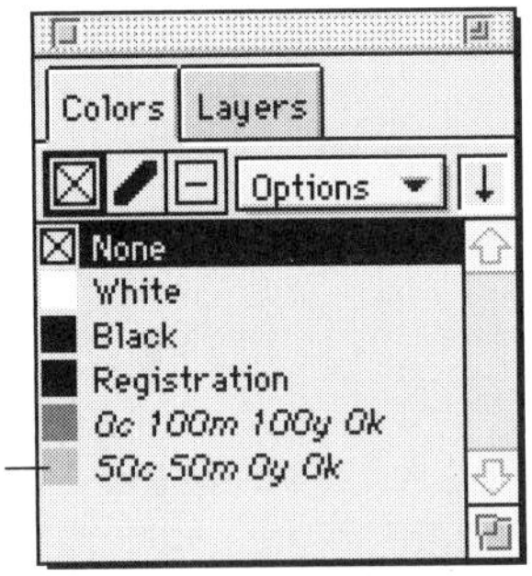

10 **Fill the shoulder and head elements with your blue color by dragging the blue color swatch from the Color List and dropping it on each of those elements.**

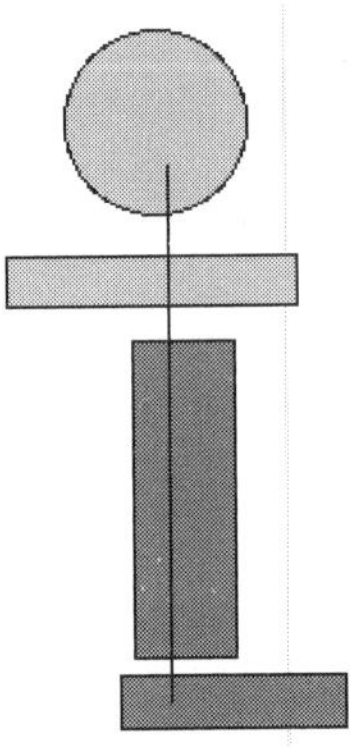

Next you will create **tints** of these colors. Tints are screens or percentages of a base color.

11 In the Color Mixer, click the Tint button to display the tint controls. Drag the red swatch from the Color List and drop it on the Base Color swatch at the top of the Tint panel.

Tints appear in 10 percent increments below the base color.

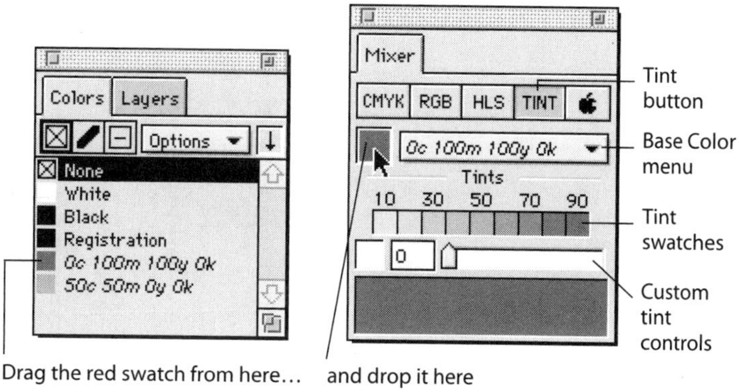

12 Drag the 30 percent swatch from the Tints panel and drop it on an empty part of the Color List.

This tint is added to the Color List.

13 Change the base color for the next tint to your blue color by choosing it from the Base Color menu.

This menu displays all of the colors in the Color List.

14 Enter *25* in the Custom Tint field to create a 25 percent tint.

By entering a value in this field, you can create a tint using any percentage, rather that just using the 10 percent increments provided by the tint swatches.

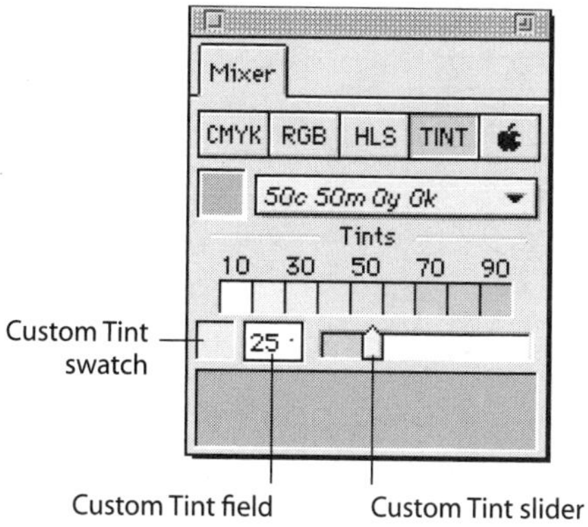

15 **Drag the custom tint swatch and drop it onto the Add Color arrow at the top of the Color List.**

This is another way to add colors to the list and is especially useful as your list of colors grows.

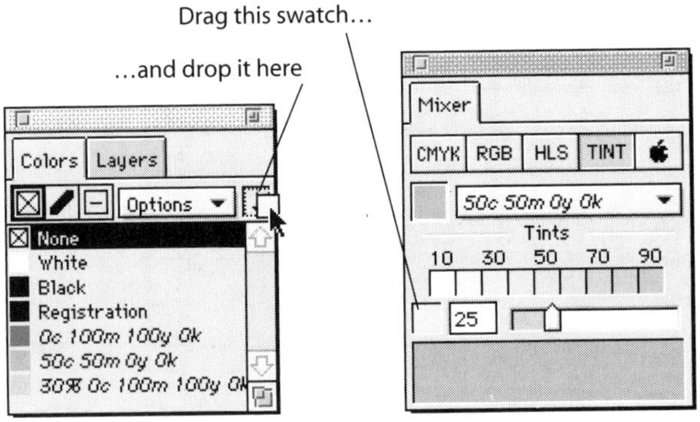

16 **Close the Color Mixer. Then display the Object Inspector by clicking its button on the toolbar.**

You have created all of the colors and tints you need at this time.

17 **Select the body rectangle on the page by clicking it with the Pointer tool. Then click the Fill Inspector tab at the top of the Inspector panel group to display the Fill controls.**

The Fill Inspector indicates that this element currently has a Basic red fill.

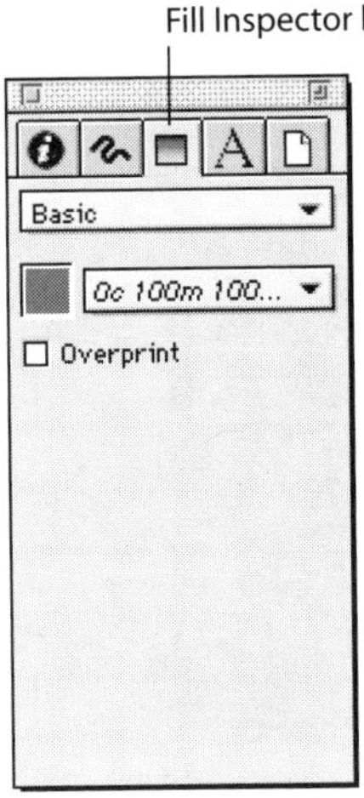

18 Change the type of fill to Gradient by using the Fill Type menu at the top of the Inspector.

The rectangle now contains a linear gradient going from red at the top to white at the bottom.

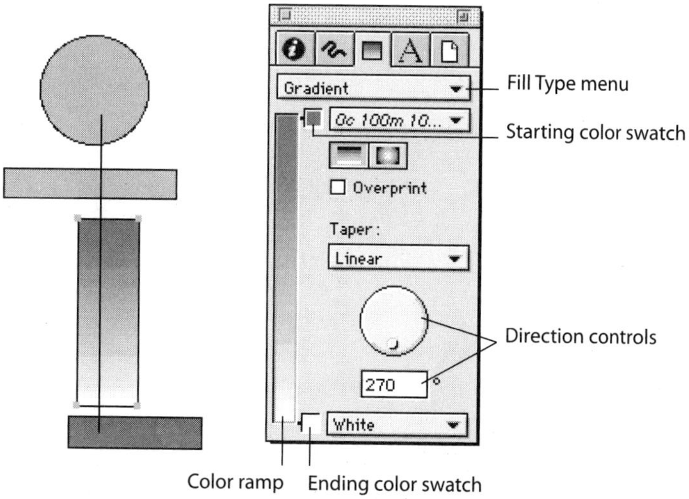

19 Drag the 30% red swatch from the Color List and drop it on the white swatch at the bottom of the Fill Inspector.

The gradient now goes from red at the top to 30% red at the bottom.

20 Drag the direction wheel or enter a new angle in the Direction field and press Enter (Windows) or Return (Macintosh).

This control allows you to change the direction of the gradient in the selected element. You can also choose between two types of fill: linear, which you used in the rectangle, and radial, which works well with rounded objects such as the robot's head.

21 Select the head and change the Fill Type to gradient. Then click the Radial button and move the center point of the radial fill slightly up and to the right by dragging the center point control in the preview at the bottom of the Inspector.

Instead of a linear gradient, this fills the circle with a radial fill, with colors radiating out from the a center point.

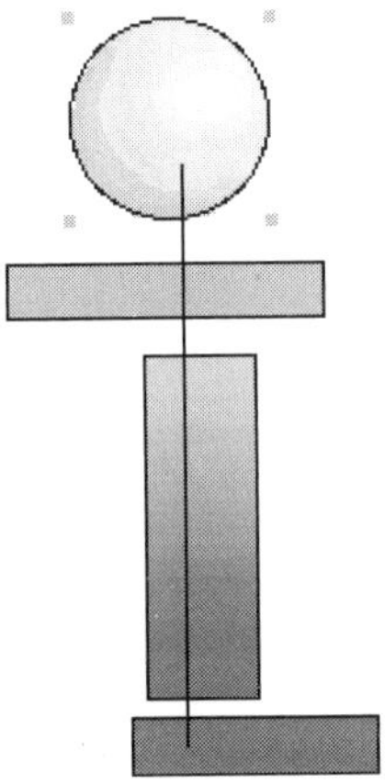

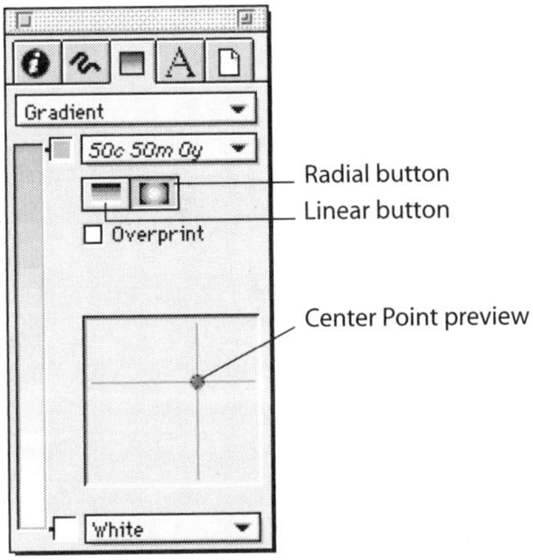

22 Select the vertical line that will be the spine of the robot and display the Stroke Inspector by clicking its tab at the top of the Inspector panel group.

The stroke characteristics for the selected line are displayed.

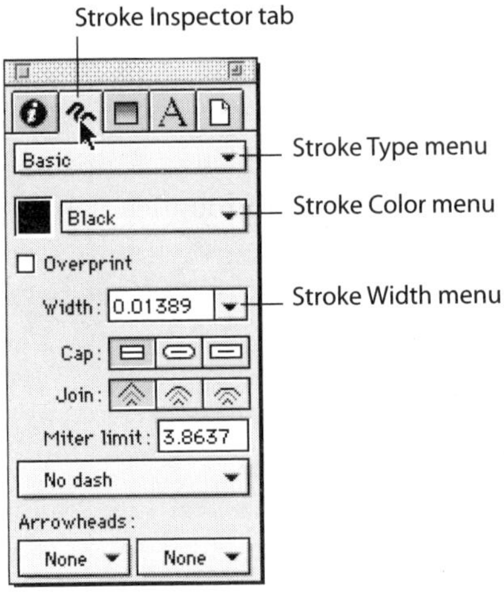

23 Change the stroke width by selecting 4 points from the Stroke Width menu.

When you release the mouse, the width is displayed in inches in the Inspector, because inches are set as the measurement units for this document.

Next you will remove the strokes around the other four elements on the page.

24 Select the head and then hold down Shift and click once on each of the three rectangles to select all of these elements at the same time.

Remember that holding Shift while clicking additional elements adds those elements to the selection.

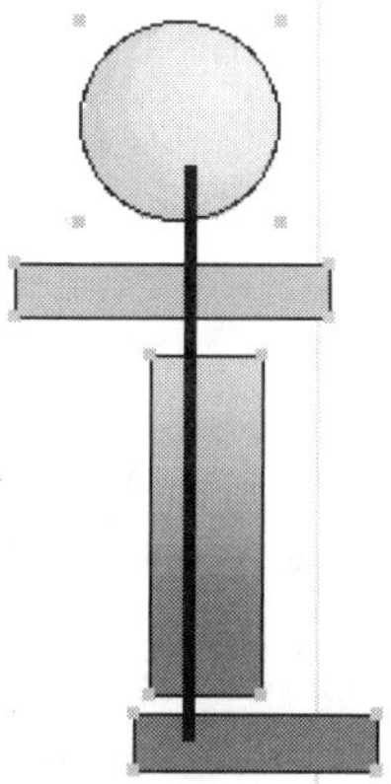

25 Change the Stroke Type from Basic to None in the Stroke Inspector and then press Tab to deselect all elements.

Now you'll make a few more changes to the gradient fill in the body rectangle.

26 Select the body rectangle and display the Fill Inspector by clicking its tab at the top of the Inspector panel group.

You will change the colors along the color ramp at the left of the Fill Inspector to modify the gradient fill.

27 Change the color of the swatch at the bottom of the Inspector to blue.

Now the gradient goes from red to blue.

28 Drag the 30 percent red color swatch from the Color List and drop it on the middle of the color ramp in the Fill Inspector. Repeat this process to add another color or tint from the Color List to the gradient.

You can create gradients that include up to 32 colors by adding more color swatches to the color ramp.

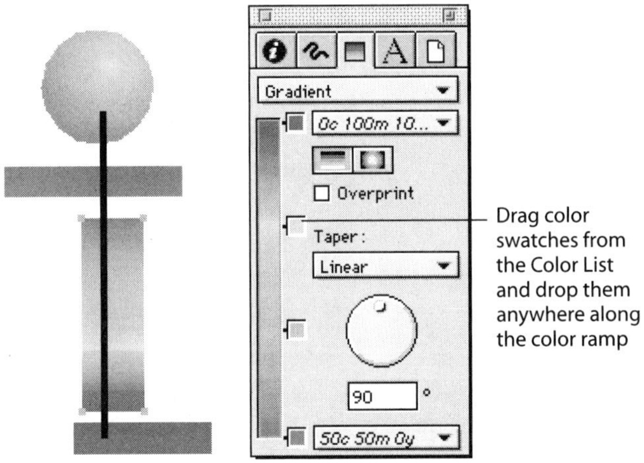

29 To remove a color from the gradient, drag the swatch out of the Inspector and release it on an empty part of the document window.

Don't release the color swatch on any element, or you may change the color of that element!

30 Move a color swatch up or down along the color ramp to adjust its position within the gradient.

In this way you can adjust the position of each color within the gradient.

31 Close both panels and press Tab to deselect the artwork.

You have completed this lesson and are ready to return to the tutorial.

32 Choose File > Exit (Windows) or File > Quit (Macintosh).

If you opened this lesson file from within the interactive tutorial, you will be returned to the tutorial automatically. Otherwise, you can return to the tutorial by double-clicking the Instruct icon on the CD.

Lesson 2-4

Working with Groups of Elements

In this lesson, you will organize, align, and group elements together.

1 **If the practice lesson 2-4 isn't open, go to the Lessons folder on the CD and open the file named 2-4.fh7.**
This document contains five basic shapes for your robot, with fills and strokes like the ones you applied in Lesson 2-3. First you will align these elements to one another so your robot will be a bit more coordinated.

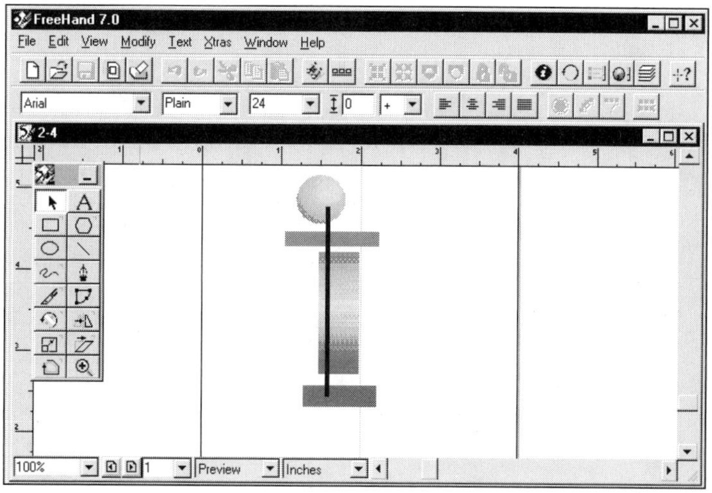

2 **Choose Edit > Select > All to select all of the elements on this page.**

3 **Display the Align panel by clicking its button on the toolbar or by choosing Window > Panels > Align.**
This panel provides several choices for both horizontal and vertical alignment.

4 **In the Vertical Alignment menu, select No Change. In the Horizontal Alignment menu, select Align Center.**

The preview display in the Align panel should show the desired results: elements centered horizontally without changing their position vertically.

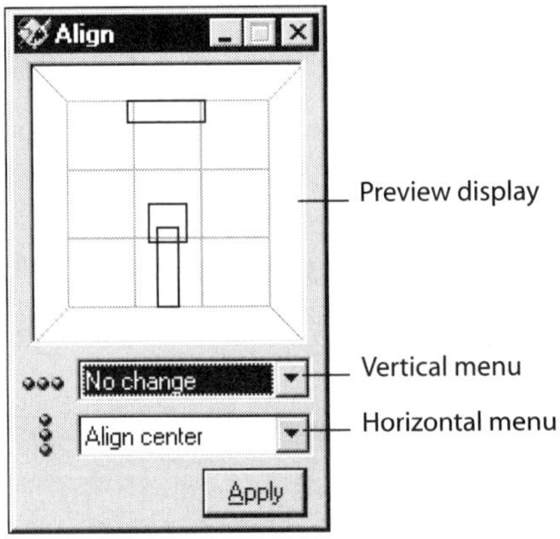

5 **Click the button at the bottom of the Align panel to align your elements. Then close the Align panel.**

All five elements are now aligned accurately.

6 **Press Tab to make sure that nothing is selected and then use the Pointer tool to select the spine.**

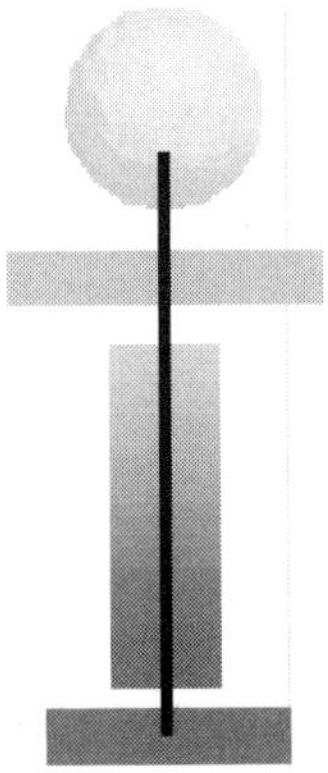

FreeHand arranges elements on the page in the order that they are created, which is why the spine of the robot is in front of the other body parts. You will now correct that by moving the spine.

7 **Choose Modify > Arrange > Send to Back.**
The spine is now behind the other elements. The Arrange menu offers four commands you can use in different situations. Use Send to Back or Bring to Front to move an object behind or in front of all of the other elements. Move Forward and Move Backward move a selected object forward or backward one element at a time.

All five elements are now arranged accurately. To keep them in this arrangement and prevent accidental changes, you can group the elements.

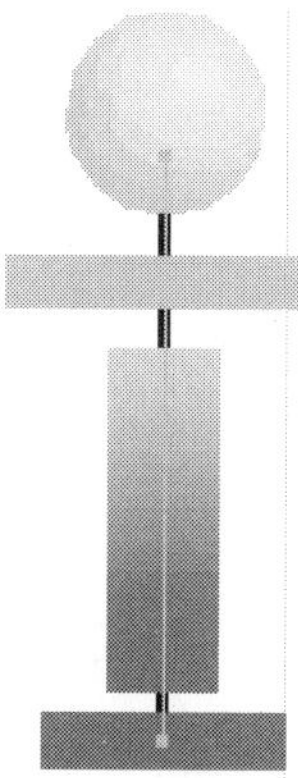

8 **Choose Edit > Select > All and then click the Group button on the toolbar or choose Modify > Group.**
This ties all the selected elements together into one group. One set of selection boxes now appears around the group, instead of individual selection boxes around each element. Now you can move, resize, and modify all of these elements as one.

9 **Move the group by positioning the Pointer tool on the spine and dragging toward the ruler guide in the center of the page. When the Pointer nears the guide, the artwork will snap into position.**
FreeHand snaps artwork to the ruler guides to help you position elements accurately on the page. Your robot is now centered on the page.

You have completed this lesson and are ready to return to the tutorial.

10 **Choose File > Exit (Windows) or File > Quit (Macintosh).**
If you opened this lesson file from within the interactive tutorial, you will be returned to the tutorial automatically. Otherwise, you can return to the tutorial by double-clicking the Instruct icon on the CD.

Lesson 2-5

Using the Transformation Tools

In this lesson, you will duplicate and transform an element to complete the robot figure.

1 **If the practice lesson 2-5 isn't open, go to the Lessons folder on the CD and open the file named 2-5.fh7.**
A few other parts of the robot figure have been added for you. The robot is almost complete, except that it is missing one leg.

2 **Choose the Magnify tool from the toolbox and drag it to surround the lower part of the robot's body.**

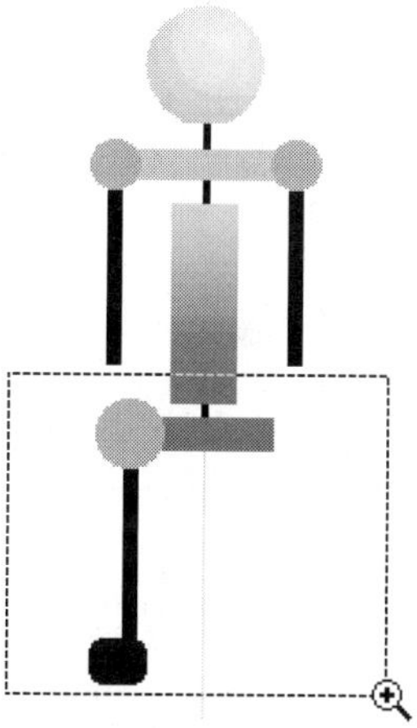

When you release the mouse button, FreeHand zooms in to the area you surrounded with the Magnify tool.

3 **Select the existing leg with the Pointer tool.**
This leg is a group of three elements. You will use the Reflect tool to position a copy of this leg on the other side of the body.

4 **Choose Edit > Clone.**
The Clone command makes a duplicate of the selected object and positions it directly in front of the original object.

5 **Choose the Reflect tool from the toolbox. Position the cursor on the ruler guide in the center of the page.**
By positioning the cursor on this guide, you ensure that the new leg will be reflected the same distance from the center of the robot as the original.

6 **Hold down the mouse button and drag downward slightly to define a reflection axis. Press Shift to constrain the reflection axis so it is perfectly vertical, so the leg will not be positioned at an angle. When the new leg appears in the correct position, release the mouse button and then the Shift key.**

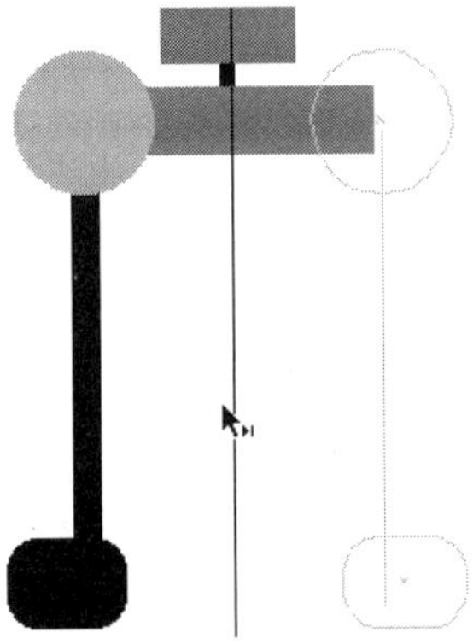

Now that the robot has two legs, you can help it jump for joy!

7 **Choose the Rotate tool in the toolbox and position the cursor at the approximate center of the circle at the top of the selected leg.**
The position of the Rotate tool cursor determines the point that the element will be rotated around.

8 Hold down the mouse button and drag the mouse out to the right along the lever that appears. Then drag upward to swing the leg out; release the mouse when you are happy with the leg's position.

The farther out along this lever you drag, the more control you will have over the rotation.

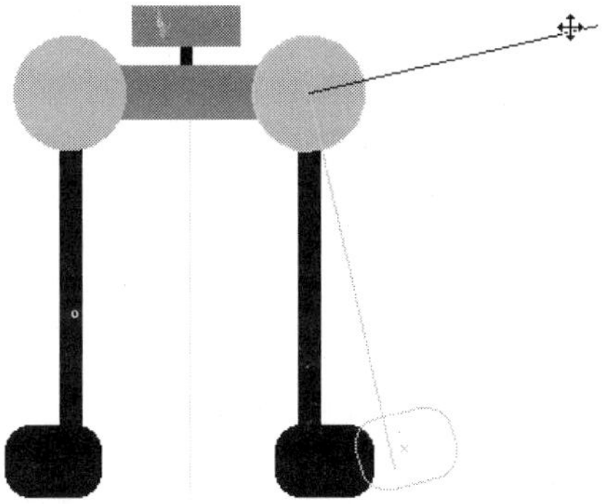

9 Choose View > Fit To Page to see the entire robot.

You have completed this lesson and are ready to return to the tutorial.

10 Choose File > Exit (Windows) or File > Quit (Macintosh).

If you opened this lesson file from within the interactive tutorial, you will be returned to the tutorial automatically. Otherwise, you can return to the tutorial by double-clicking the Instruct icon on the CD.

3 Working with Paths and Points

This section consists of three lessons:

- Manipulating Points and Paths
- Creating New Paths with the Bezigon Tool
- Creating New Paths with the Pen Tool

Graphics in FreeHand are made up of **paths**, which are lines containing at least two points. The span between two points, either straight or curved, is a **path segment**.

As you will see in this section, you can manipulate these paths, also known as **Bézier curves**, to create virtually any shape and to make precise adjustments to those shapes.

Lesson 3-1

Manipulating Points and Paths

To see points and paths in action, you will start by drawing a basic shape.

1 **If the practice lesson 3-1 isn't open, go to the Lessons folder on the CD and open the file named 3-1.fh7.**
This document contains one empty letter-size page.

2 **Choose the Rectangle tool from the toolbox and draw a rectangle on the page.**
You can create any size of rectangle on any part of the page.

3 **With the Pointer tool, resize the rectangle by dragging one of its selection boxes.**
An element created with the Rectangle or Ellipse tool is a **grouped path**, and you can resize it as a basic shape as long as it remains grouped.

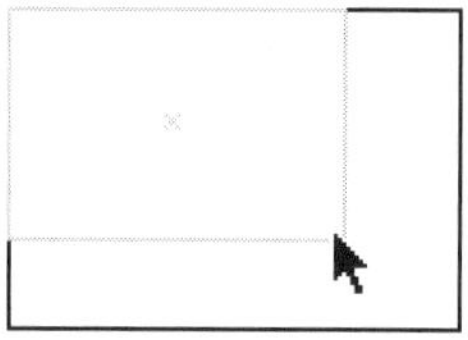

4 **Click the Ungroup button on the toolbar or choose Modify > Ungroup.**
The sides of the shape now appear selected, as do the selection boxes.

5 **Use the Pointer tool to drag the same corner selection box outward.**
You are now adjusting the position of that individual **point** on the path, rather than resizing the rectangle.

In addition to adjusting the positions of the existing points on this path, you can add new ones.

6 **Click the Bezigon tool in the toolbox. Position the cursor along a segment of the selected path and click the mouse.**
You have just added a point to this path.

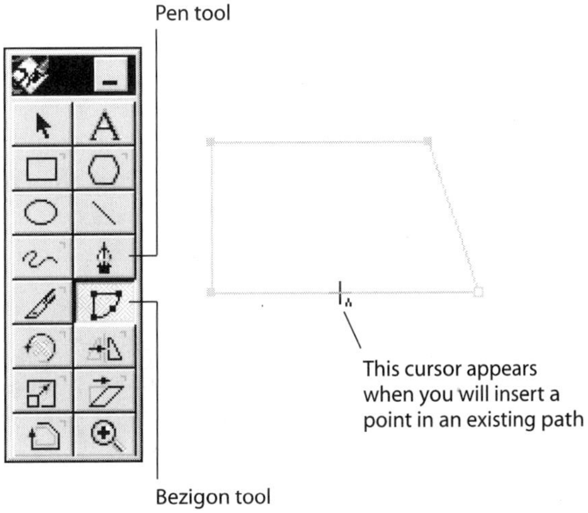

7 **Switch back to the Pointer tool and move the new point to a different position.**
The five points on this path are all **corner points**, and are displayed as squares when the path is selected. FreeHand paths can also contain **curve points**, so you can create both smooth curves and straight segments in your artwork.

The newest point on your path appears as an outlined square, which indicates that it is selected.

8 Display the Object Inspector by clicking its button on the toolbar or by choosing Window > Inspectors > Object.

The Object Inspector displays information about the selected path and point.

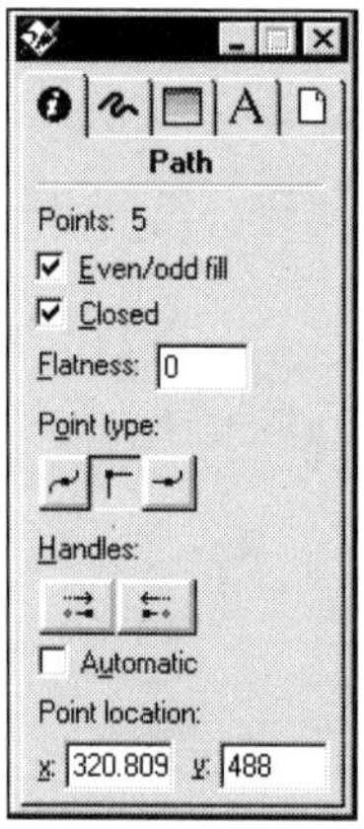

9 Click the Curve Point button in the Object Inspector to change the selected point from a corner point to a curve point.

The path does not change visibly—yet.

10 Click Automatic in the Object Inspector.

FreeHand automatically adjusts the path so it follows a smooth curve through your curve point. Two **control handles** now extend from that selected point; you can adjust these handles to change the curve.

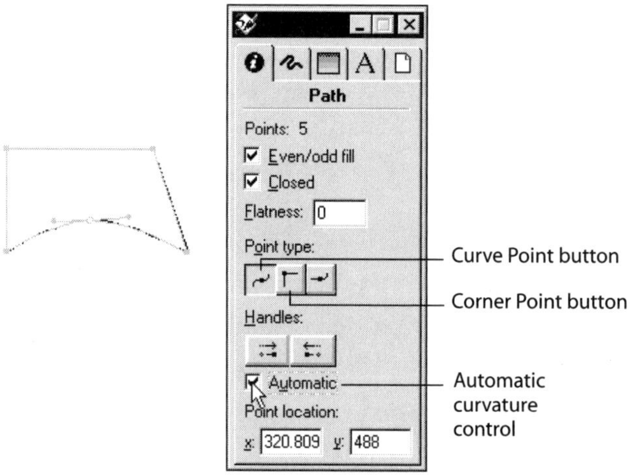

11 Drag the left control handle downward with the Pointer tool.

As the left control handle goes down, the right control handle goes up. Control handles for curve points are connected to one another, like a long lever. By changing the length and direction of the control handles, you can change the direction of the path as it passes through the selected point.

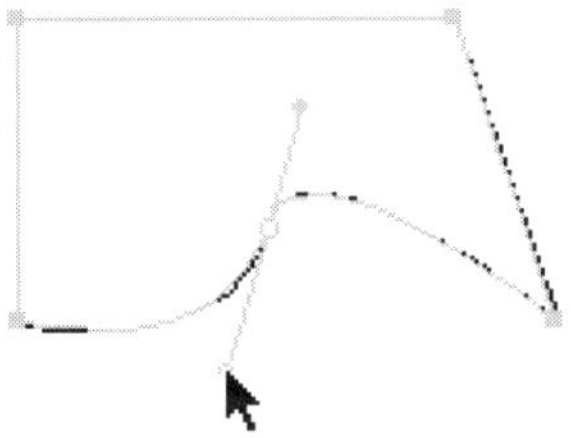

12 Click the Pointer tool on a different point along the path to select that point.

When a point is selected, you can move it, change its type, modify its control handles, or delete it.

13 Press Delete on the keyboard to remove this point from the path.

Now the Object Inspector indicates that this path contains four points.

14 Use the Ellipse tool to add an ellipse somewhere on the page. Then ungroup this basic shape so you can modify this path directly.

To ungroup, you choose Modify > Ungroup or click the Ungroup button on the toolbar. Now there are four points on this path that you can move and manipulate with the Pointer tool.

15 Click a point with the Pointer and then press Delete.

The point is removed.

16 Click a segment of a path to select that path and then press Delete. Select the other path on this page and press Delete.

The paths are deleted.

As you can see, one way to create custom paths is to ungroup and modify basic shapes. Now you'll try some other ways to create complex paths.

17 Draw an ellipse on the page. Then draw a rectangle that partially overlaps the ellipse.

Make sure your elements touch one another so you will clearly see the results of the next steps.

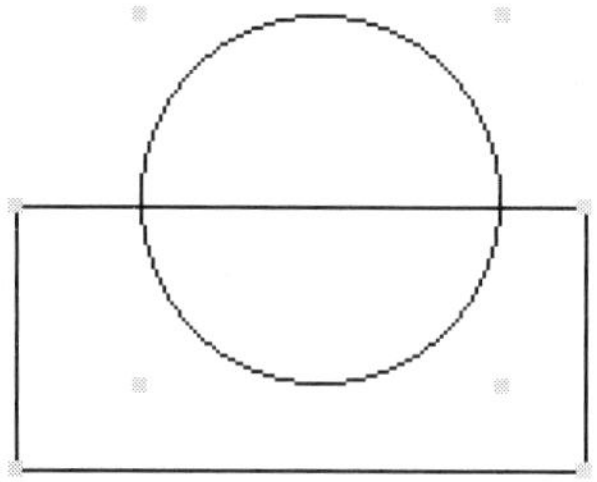

18 Select one of the elements on the page with the Pointer tool and then hold down Shift and click the other element to add it to the selection.

You will combine these two selected elements into one path using FreeHand's path operations, so they will no longer be two individual shapes.

19 Choose Modify > Combine > Union.

This combines the entire area of each path together into one new path.

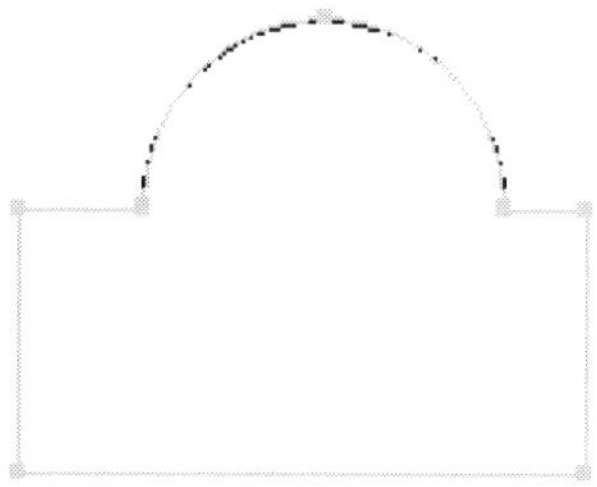

20 Choose Edit > Undo to try a different option.

Your two selected shapes appear again.

21 Choose Modify > Combine > Intersect.

A path is created where the two original paths overlapped.

22 Choose Undo again to try one other choice.

23 Choose Modify > Combine > Punch.

This subtracts the object in front from the object behind it. Since you created the rectangle after drawing the ellipse, the rectangle was in front of the ellipse. In this example, the Punch command leaves the part of the ellipse that is not covered by the rectangle.

In the next two lessons, you will learn how to create new paths from scratch.

You have completed this lesson and are ready to return to the tutorial.

24 Choose File > Exit (Windows) or File > Quit (Macintosh).

If you opened this lesson file from within the interactive tutorial, you will be returned to the tutorial automatically. Otherwise, you can return to the tutorial by double-clicking the Instruct icon on the CD.

Lesson 3-2

Creating New Paths with the Bezigon Tool

In this lesson, you will use the Bezigon tool to create and modify paths. You can use this tool to create all kinds of paths, from shapes with pointed corners to smooth, fluid curves.

1 **If the practice lesson 3-2 isn't open, go to the Lessons folder on the CD and open the file named 3-2.fh7.**
This document contains several graphics in the background for you to trace with the Bezigon tool. Tracing these simple shapes will show you how you can create any type of curve or straight line by positioning corner and curve points.

2 **Select the Bezigon tool in the toolbox.**
First you will create a simple triangle on an empty part of the page.

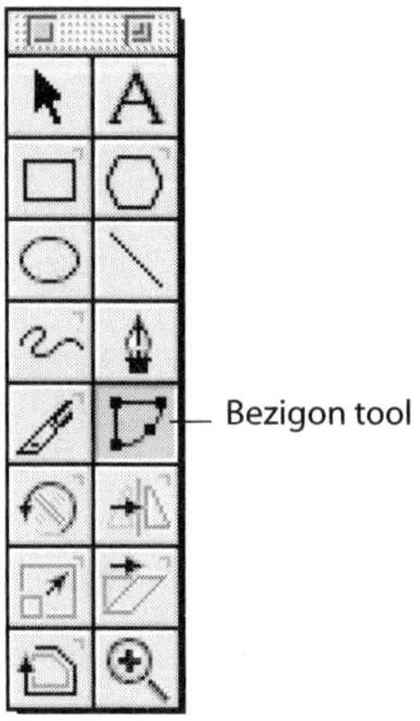

3 **Click once to start a new path by placing a corner point. Then click to create two more corner points, to create a triangle. Close the path by clicking the starting point again.**
You can create either open or closed paths. However, you can apply a fill only to closed paths.

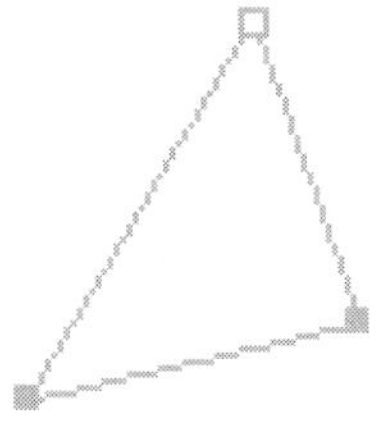

Now begin tracing the boat.

Tip: Watch the cursor as you create paths. The crosshair cursor is displayed with an empty square alongside it when you are ready to create a new path. The crosshair appears with a small caret beside it when you can add points to an active path. A solid square appears near the crosshair when the mouse is positioned over the first point in the path, so you know that clicking that point will close the path.

4 **Click to place a corner point at the top rear corner of the boat.**
You will work your way around this pattern in a clockwise direction.

5 **Hold Shift and click the second point, at the base of the triangular sail.**
Holding Shift when you click the point that completes a segment constrains that segment to be perfectly vertical, horizontal, or at a 45-degree angle.

6 **Click the next point, then the next, and continue around the pattern clicking to place each corner point. Finally, click on the starting point to complete the shape by closing the path.**
Always trace around the shape—do not jump across the tracing pattern as you work. Remember to hold Shift when clicking to complete the horizontal and vertical segments in this boat.

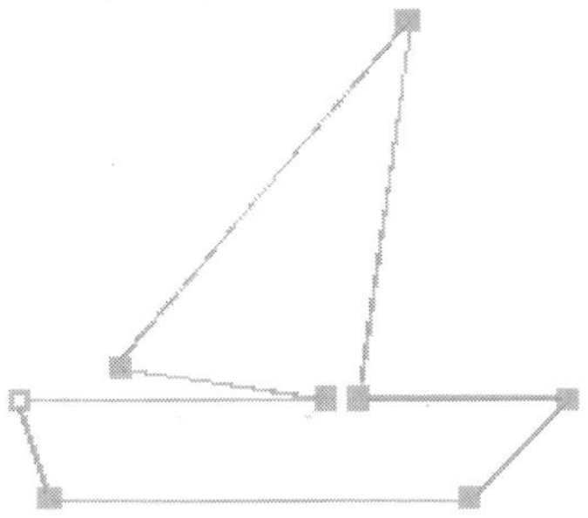

7 **Begin tracing the next pattern, a billowing sail, by clicking a corner point at the top of the sail.**
Tracing this sail will require curve points, which you can also place with the Bezigon tool.

8 **Add a curve point at the outermost part of the outer curve by holding down Alt (Windows) or Option (Macintosh) and clicking the mouse.**
The path won't look like a curve until you add the next point.

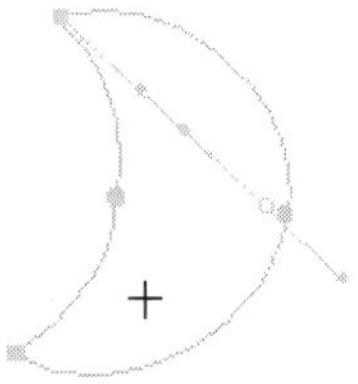

9 **Without holding down any key on the keyboard, click to add a corner point at the bottom of the sail.**
The path automatically adjusts to become a smooth curve.

10 **Add another curve point by holding down Alt (Windows) or Option (Macintosh) and clicking the mouse at the outermost point along the inner curve. Then close the path by clicking the original point again.**
Once the path is complete, you can use the Pointer tool to make adjustments as needed.

11 Display the Color List. Drag color swatches of your choice and drop them on the boat and sail paths to fill each with color.

Next you will position the billowing sail on the boat.

12 Use the Pointer tool to move the sail into position over the boat. Then press Tab to deselect all of the elements.

You can move the filled sail by pointing to its middle and dragging. You would need to point to the outline of the shape if it had no fill, since the middle is empty without a fill.

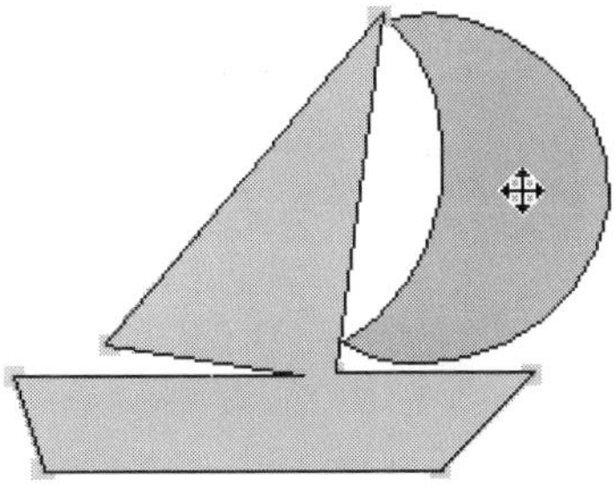

Now try tracing another pattern.

13 Scroll down to see the entire fish tracing pattern in this document.

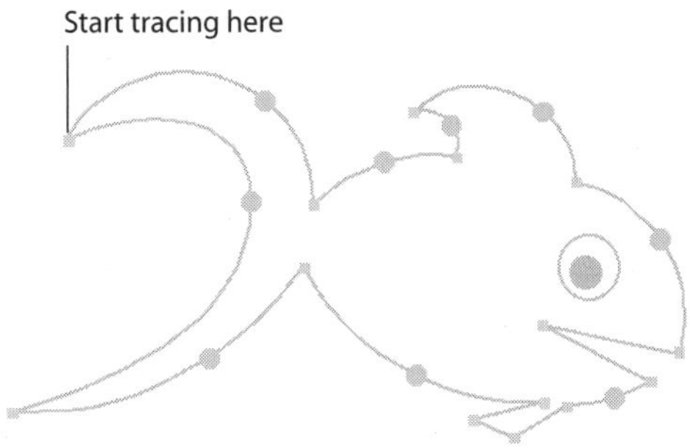

14 Choose the Bezigon tool again and begin a new path by clicking a corner point at the upper tip of the tail.

The small squares along the fish's outline indicate where you should position corner points. Place curve points on the small circles in this tracing pattern.

15 Work your way around the fish, adding curve and corner points as needed. When you're finished, close the path by clicking the first point again.

Remember to work around the shape as you trace. Don't worry if the path does not match the tracing pattern exactly—it's better to complete the path and then adjust it with the Pointer tool than to stop along the way.

When you close the path, the tail of your fish looks terrible.

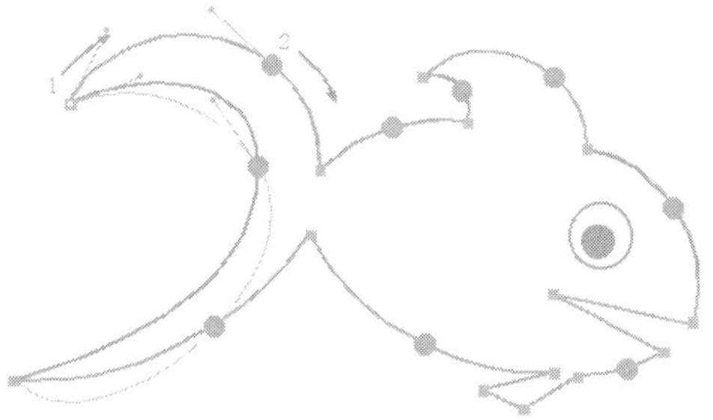

16 Switch back to the Pointer tool. Click the curve point in the middle of the tail to select it.

The control handles for this curve point are at an angle, but at this precise point the path should be headed straight up.

17 Point to the top handle and drag to adjust the control handles so they're vertical.

The segment above this point should now closely follow the tracing pattern. The bottom part of the tail still needs some work, however. You can also fine-tune a path segment by adjusting the control handle on the point at the opposite end of the segment.

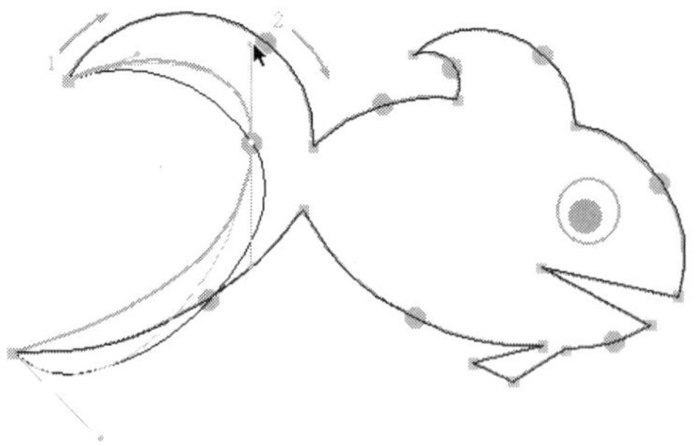

18 Select the point at the bottom of the tail.

A control handle extends down and to the right, which is why the path heads in this direction.

Note: Corner points can also have two control handles. Unlike curve points, though, the control handles for corner points are not connected to one another — they can be moved independently.

19 Adjust the control handle on the bottom tail point so it points up and to the right and change its distance from the point as needed to adjust the path segment to match the tracing pattern.

With these adjustments, you have now created a nice smooth path for this fish.

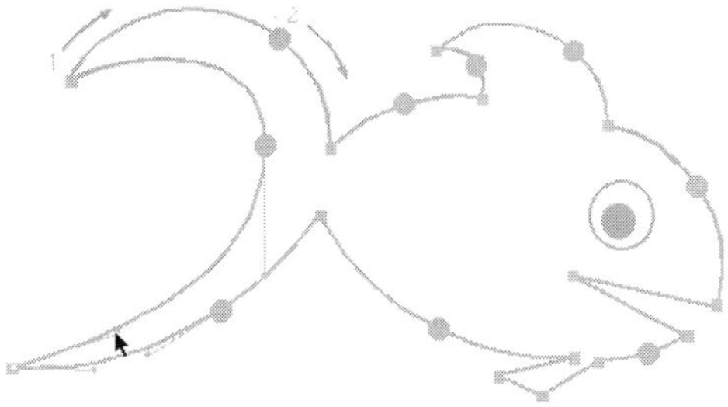

You have completed this lesson and are ready to return to the tutorial.

20 Choose File > Exit (Windows) or File > Quit (Macintosh).

If you opened this lesson file from within the interactive tutorial, you will be returned to the tutorial automatically. Otherwise, you can return to the tutorial by double-clicking the Instruct icon on the CD.

Lesson 3-3

Creating New Paths with the Pen Tool

The Pen tool offers another way for you to create points and paths.

1 **If the practice lesson 3-3 isn't open, go to the Lessons folder on the CD and open the file named 3-3.fh7.**
This document contains patterns you will trace with the Pen tool. You will start by tracing a curving line.

2 **Choose the Pen tool in the toolbox and position it on the first point in the top tracing pattern.**

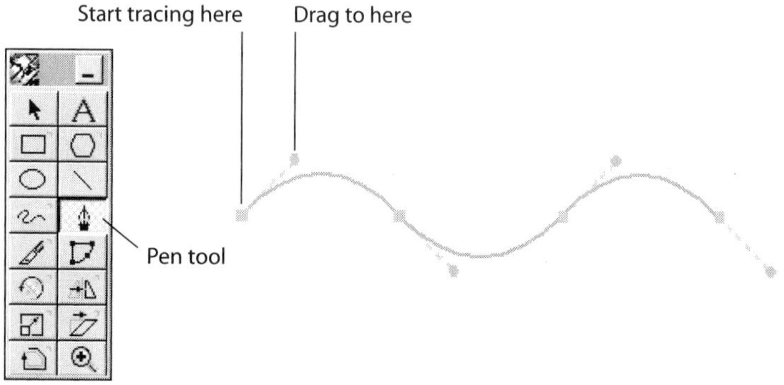

When you use the Pen tool, you click to place a corner point. To create a curve point, you hold and drag the mouse to pull control handles out of the new point you are adding in the direction you want the path to head from that point.

3 **Hold down the mouse button and drag up and to the right to pull out the control handles for this curve point. Release the mouse when the cursor is positioned over the red dot in the tracing pattern.**
Unlike with the Bezigon tool, with the Pen tool you manually position all of the control handles to define curved paths.

4 **Move to the next point and drag down and to the right, since the path should be headed that way as it enters this point.**

To determine the direction to drag the control handles, imagine that you are tracing the pattern with a pencil. The direction that the pencil would be moving when it *touches* a point is the direction that the control handles must follow for that point.

5 **Continue along the path, adding curve points by dragging out the curve handles in the direction the path should head at each point.**

6 **When you have completed the path, press the Tab key to deselect the artwork.**

Since this is an open path, you must deselect it before starting to trace another path on this page. Otherwise the next point you click will be another point on this path, rather than the beginning point on a new path.

Now you will use the Pen tool to trace the same fish that you traced with the Bezigon tool in Lesson 3-2.

7 **Scroll down to see the entire fish pattern.**

The tracing pattern identifies the positions of the points you need to create this path.

8 **Position the Pen tool cursor at the upper tip of the tail. Hold down the mouse and drag up and to the right (as indicated by the template).**

The next point you need is at the end of this curve over the top of the tail.

9 **Point to the next spot along the tracing pattern. Drag straight down—but do not release the mouse.**

By pulling downward from this point, you can adjust the curve over the top of the tail so that it matches the tracing pattern. But the path should not continue in this direction as it leaves this point—you will have to disconnect the control handles so you can adjust the one that controls the path as it comes out of this point.

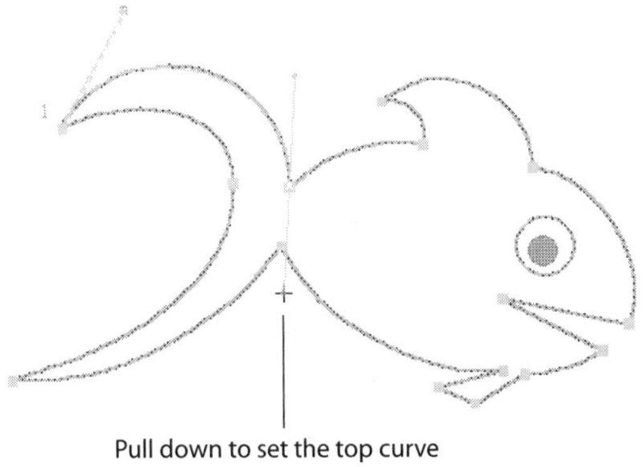

10 **After you pull the handle downward to define the curve over the top of the tail correctly, hold down Alt (Windows) or Option (Macintosh) and move the control handle up and to the right, to direct the path along the next segment.**

Holding the Alt or Option key while adding a point allows you to disconnect the control handles and point them in different directions.

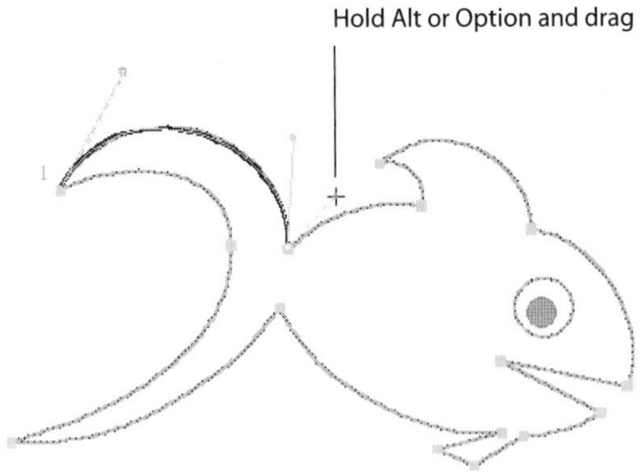

11 Continue working your way around the fish pattern, holding Alt (Windows) or Option (Macintosh) any time you want to change the direction of the path segment coming out of the point you are adding.

Don't worry if you path does not match the pattern exactly. You can use the Pointer tool to adjust the path after it is completed.

12 To close this path, click once more on the original point.

You do not need to hold down any keys on the keyboard.

13 Using the Pointer tool, swing the last control handle to the correct direction to complete the fish.

14 Press Tab or click off of the path to deselect all elements so you can see your results.

As you have seen in this lesson and the previous one, both the Pen and Bezigon tools can be used to create the same kinds of shapes. The choice between the two is a personal one. It is a good idea to practice using both tools; as you become more familiar with the tools, your preference may change!

You have completed this lesson and are ready to return to the tutorial.

15 Choose File > Exit (Windows) or File > Quit (Macintosh).

If you opened this lesson file from within the interactive tutorial, you will be returned to the tutorial automatically. Otherwise, you can return to the tutorial by double-clicking the Instruct icon on the CD.

4 Working with Text

This section consists of four lessons:

- Entering and Editing Text
- Formatting Text
- Attaching Text to a Path
- Converting Text to Paths

In addition to providing tools you can use to create sophisticated graphics, FreeHand also offers you extensive controls for entering, editing, and formatting text in your layouts. In this section you will explore these controls. You will also learn how to create special effects with type by placing text along a curve and changing text characters into graphics.

Lesson 4-1

Entering and Editing Text

You use the Text tool when you're ready to add text to your layout.

1 **If the practice lesson 4-1 isn't open, go to the Lessons folder on the CD and open the file named 4-1.fh7.**
You will now add text to this layout.

2 **Click the Text tool in the toolbox. Then click once on the page to create a new text block.**
An insertion point appears where you clicked, waiting for you to enter text.

3 **Type *Light the Way* in this text block.**
The text is entered on the page in the new text block. A text ruler appears above the text as you type.

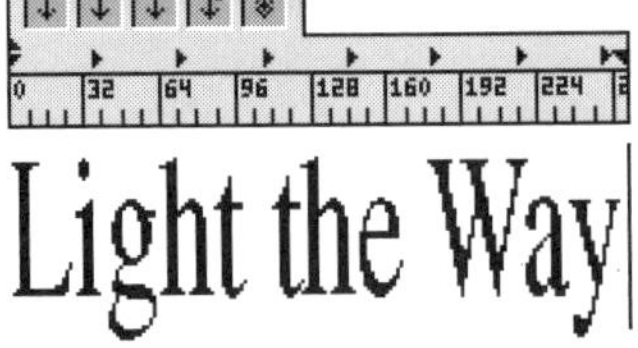

4 Choose the Pointer tool in the toolbox and click the text to select the entire text block.

This selects the text block. Because you cannot edit the text when it is selected in this way, the text ruler at the top of the text block disappears.

Tip: If you drag an element quickly, only its outline appears as you move it. However, if you hold down the mouse button and wait for a moment, a four-direction cursor appears, and you can see the actual object as you drag.

5 Move the text block by pointing to any part of the text and dragging.

Position the text as shown here.

6 Display the Color List by clicking its button on the toolbar or choosing Window > Panels > Color List.

7 Change the color of the text in this block by dragging the bright yellow color swatch from the Color List and dropping it on any part of the text.

This changes the color of all of this text. When the entire text block is selected in this way, you can change the characteristics of all text within the block.

8 Click just to the right of the word *Light* with the Text tool.

This positions the insertion point in the text block so you can enter additional information.

9 Change the first word from *Light* to *Lighting*.

The Text tool enables you to enter text into a new text block and change the contents of an existing text block.

10 Select the first word by dragging the Text tool cursor across the word. Drag the light yellow color swatch from the Color List and drop it on the selected text.

The color of the first word changes, although the text doesn't look yellow since this word is selected. As soon as you deselect the text, the yellow color will appear.

You can make changes to selected text without affecting the other characters in this text block.

11 Click an empty part of the page or pasteboard with the Pointer tool to deselect all text.

Do not press Tab to deselect when you are editing a text block—that would insert a tab character instead!

You have completed this lesson and are ready to return to the tutorial.

12 Choose File > Exit (Windows) or File > Quit (Macintosh).

If you opened this lesson file from within the interactive tutorial, you will be returned to the tutorial automatically. Otherwise, you can return to the tutorial by double-clicking the Instruct icon on the CD.

Lesson 4-2

Formatting Text

You will now format the characters in the two text blocks on the Robotz Toys page.

1 **If the practice lesson 4-2 isn't open, go to the Lessons folder on the CD and open the file named 4-2.fh7.**

2 **With the Pointer tool, click the top text block on the page to select it.**
When a text block is selected with the Pointer tool, you can change the characteristics of all text within the block.

Note: If the fonts used in this lesson are not available on your system, choose any font available to format the text.

3 **Using the controls on the text toolbar, change the font to Arial (Windows) or Helvetica (Macintosh), change the type style to bold, and change the size to 48 points.**
The text toolbar provides easy access to these and other text formatting controls.

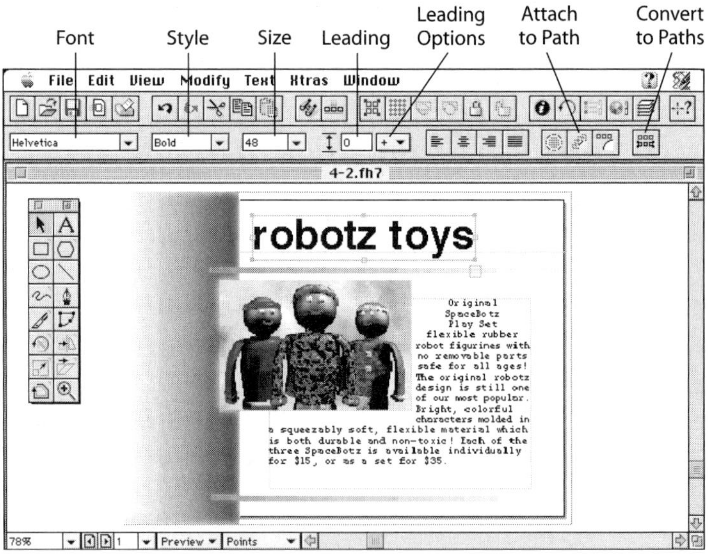

You can also use the Text Inspector to format your text.

4 **Display the Text Inspector by choosing Window > Inspectors > Text.**

Alternatively, you can click the Object Inspector button on the toolbar and then click the Text Inspector tab at the top of the Inspector panel group.

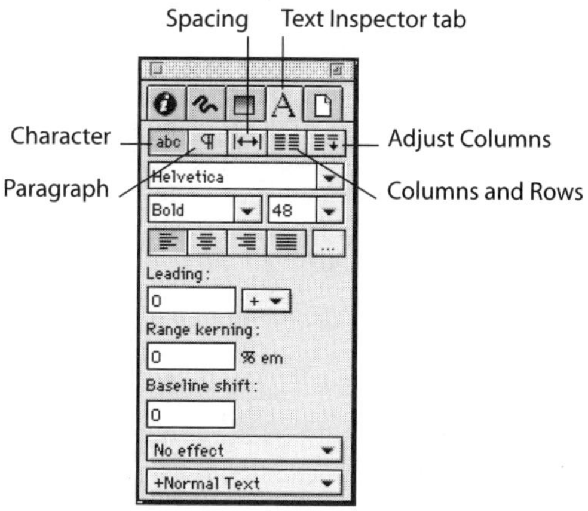

The Text Inspector has five sets of controls, which you access by clicking one of the five buttons at the top.

5 **Click the Character button at the top left of the Inspector and type *15* in the Range Kerning field. Then press Enter (Windows) or Return (Macintosh).**

Range Kerning adjusts the space between individual characters. A positive value, such as the 15 you entered here, loosens the text by adding space between characters. Enter a negative value when you want to tighten the text by reducing the space between the characters.

Note: The character controls in the Text Inspector include the same font, size, leading, and alignment controls you can find in the text toolbar. All of these text formatting controls are also available from the Text menu. These three choices enable you to work with these controls in the way that's best for you.

Range kerning changes the space between the characters, but it does not alter the character shapes. To expand or condense the characters themselves, you use the Horizontal Scale control.

6 **Click the Spacing button in the Text Inspector, enter *120* in the Horizontal Scale field, and press Enter (Windows) or Return (Macintosh).**

The characters in the selected text block are now wider.

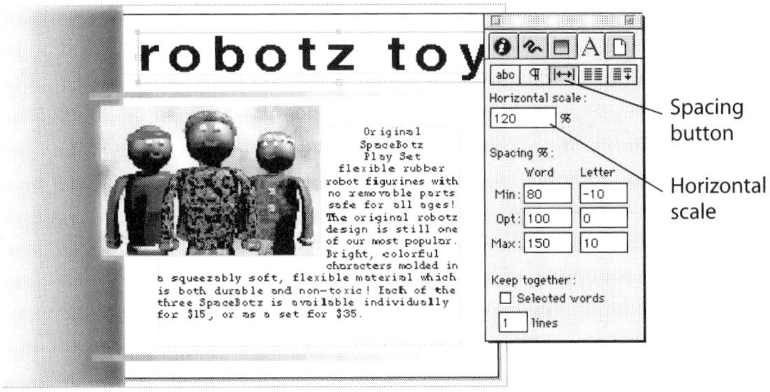

Horizontal scale controls the width of the characters. A horizontal scale value of 100 percent represents the normal character width. A larger value, such as the 120 you entered, makes the characters wider. A value less than 100 compresses the character shapes.

7 **Use the Pointer tool to move this text block so the first two characters are positioned over the purple rectangle at the left of this page.**

Position your text block similar to the one shown here.

Tip: A shortcut for selecting one word is to double-click the word with the Text tool.

8 **Double-click the text block to automatically switch to the Text tool. Select the word *toys* and change the type style to Plain.**
The change applies only to the characters you have selected.

9 **Display the Color List by clicking its button on the toolbar or choosing Window > Panels > Color List.**

10 **Select the first two characters in the word *robotz*. Drag the white swatch from the Color List and drop it on the selected characters. Then click a blank part of the page or pasteboard with the Pointer tool to deselect all elements.**
When you select characters within a text block with the Text tool, you can modify the selected text without affecting the other characters in the text block.

Now you're ready to format the text in the other text block. First you'll zoom in on that text block, so you can see the text more clearly.

11 **Select the large text block with the Pointer tool. Choose View > Magnification > 100% to see this element at actual size.**
When you have an item selected and change your view, FreeHand will center the selected item in your new view of the artwork.

12 **With the entire text block still selected, change the font to Times and the size to 10 points.**
Next you will change the vertical space, or **leading**, between the lines of text. The leading controls on the toolbar enable you to specify leading in several ways.

13 **Using the menu on the toolbar, change the leading type to percent (%). Then enter *120* in the Leading field and press Enter (Windows) or Return (Macintosh).**
The leading will now be 120 percent of the point size of your type. This setting adjusts the space between all the lines of text within the selected text block.

14 Use the Text tool to select the top three lines of text in the text block. Type *16* in the type size field on the text toolbar and press Enter (Windows) or Return (Macintosh).

As you can see, you can enter any type size directly, even if it is not available on the Type Size menu!

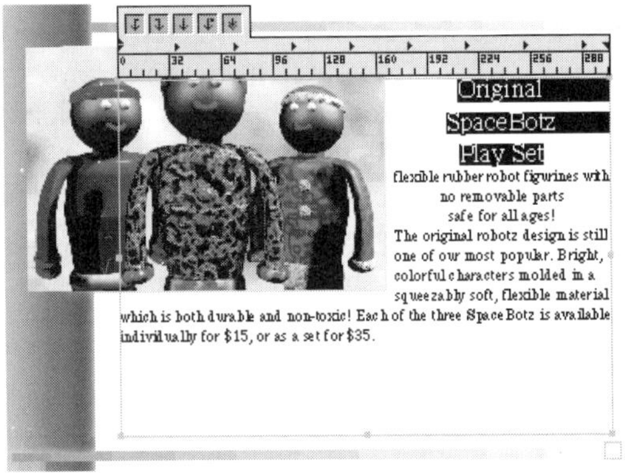

15 Select the next three lines and change the type size to 12 points.

There are actually two separate paragraphs in this selection, although it is difficult to tell right now. You will add additional space between these paragraphs to improve the appearance of this text.

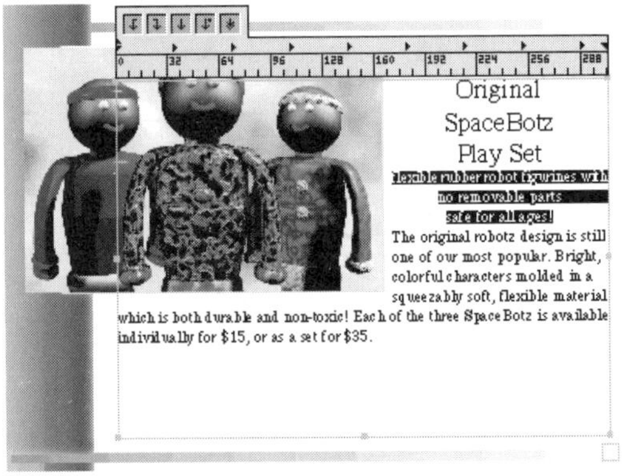

16 Click the Paragraph button in the Text Inspector. Enter a new value of *6* points in the Paragraph Spacing field that controls the space above these paragraphs.

Entering a value in the Above field in this panel adds space above each of the selected paragraphs.

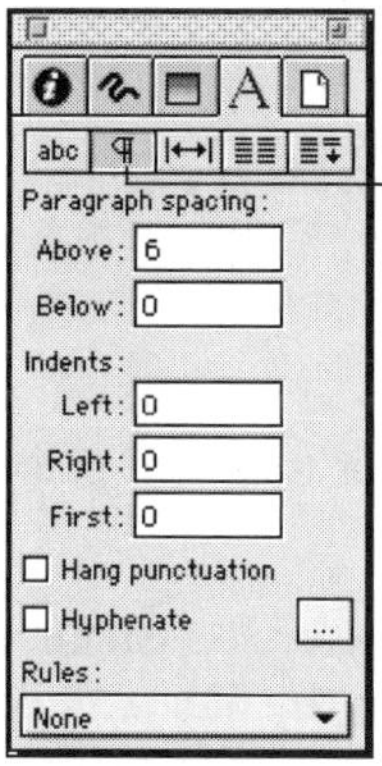

17 **Select the last paragraph with the Text tool and change the space above this paragraph to 30 points.**
This completes the formatting for these text blocks.

18 **Click the Pointer tool on an empty part of the page and choose View > Fit To Page.**
Now the page looks much better.

You have completed this lesson and are ready to return to the tutorial.

19 **Choose File > Exit (Windows) or File > Quit (Macintosh).**
If you opened this lesson file from within the interactive tutorial, you will be returned to the tutorial automatically. Otherwise, you can return to the tutorial by double-clicking the Instruct icon on the CD.

Lesson 4-3

Attaching Text to a Path

FreeHand also makes it easy to place text along a curved or straight path.

1 **If the practice lesson 4-3 isn't open, go to the Lessons folder on the CD and open the file named 4-3.fh7.**
In this document there are several text and graphic elements on the pasteboard to the right of the Robotz Toys page.

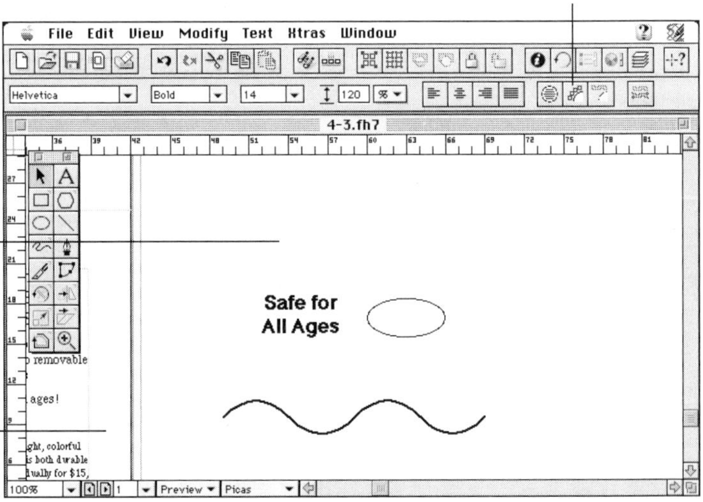

2 **Choose the Ellipse tool from the toolbox. Then hold down Shift and draw a small circle above the other elements on the screen.**
Remember to hold down Shift to draw perfect circles with the Ellipse tool.

3 **Click the Attach to Path button on the toolbar or choose Text > Attach to Path**

A text insertion point appears blinking at the top center of the circle.

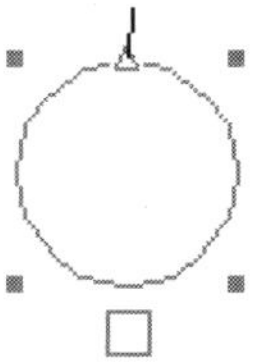

4 **Enter the text *Safe for* along the top of this circle. Then press Enter (Windows) or Return (Macintosh) and type the words *All Ages* around the bottom of the circle.**

Text that is typed after you press Enter (Windows) or Return (Macintosh) is automatically attached to the bottom of a closed path.

Attach to Path also works if you already have an existing text block and an existing path.

5 **Use the Pointer tool to select the text block just below the text on the circle you just completed. Hold down Shift and click the ellipse that is positioned just to the right of this selected text block.**

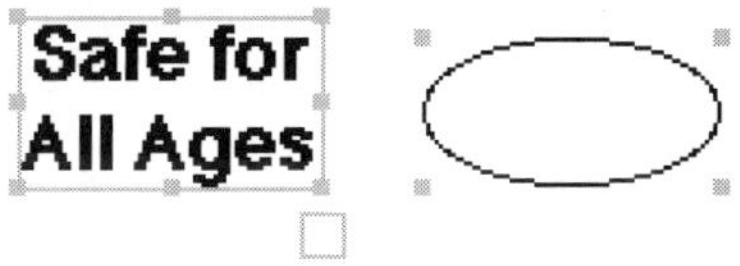

After you select both the text block and the path you want to attach it to, use the Attach to Path command just as you did before.

6 **Click the Attach to Path button on the toolbar or choose Text > Attach to Path.**

The text is automatically fit to the path.

7 **Click the Pointer tool on an empty part of the pasteboard.**

Notice that the path the text is attached to is not visible unless the element is selected. When you attach text to a path, the path disappears (and it will not print).

8 **To select that same text on a path, click directly on the text with the Pointer tool.**

FreeHand automatically rotates the characters around the path as it curves, but you can change the way the text is attached to the path.

9 **Display the Object Inspector by clicking its button on the toolbar and choose Skew Vertical from the Orientation menu.**

The characters now remain upright, with the horizontal elements of each character conforming to the shape of the path. This is one of the ways you can enhance text after it is attached to a path.

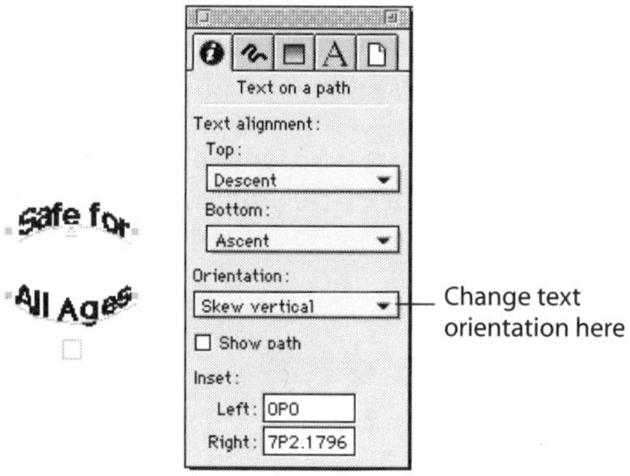

10 **Select the open path at the bottom of the screen with the Pointer tool. Click the Attach to Path button on the Text toolbar and enter *roller coaster* along the path.**

As you can see, you can attach text to open paths just as you can to closed paths.

11 **Click an empty part of the pasteboard to deselect all elements.**

Don't press Tab to deselect items when you're working with text—you may enter a tab character into the text block instead!

12 **Choose View > Magnification > 50%.**

Now you can see the page and the elements you have created on the pasteboard.

13 **Position the Pointer tool on the text that you attached to the ellipse.**

This is the element with the text orientation set to skew vertical.

14 **Drag this element onto the page. Position it near the bottom-left corner of the page and release the mouse button.**

Move text attached to a path just as you move any other text or path in your document.

15 **Deselect all elements and choose View > Fit To Page.**

You have completed this lesson and are ready to return to the tutorial.

16 **Choose File > Exit (Windows) or File > Quit (Macintosh).**

If you opened this lesson file from within the interactive tutorial, you will be returned to the tutorial automatically. Otherwise, you can return to the tutorial by double-clicking the Instruct icon on the CD.

Lesson 4-4

Converting Text to Paths

FreeHand offers you a great deal of precision and flexibility when you are working with type in your documents. However, there are a few special effects that you can apply to paths in FreeHand but not to text, such as a gradient fill. In this lesson, you will see that this doesn't mean you have to settle for plain text!

1 **If the practice lesson 4-5 isn't open, go to the Lessons folder on the CD and open the file named 4-5.fh7.**
This document contains two text blocks. You will make changes to the large text block on this page, which contains one word—*Faust*. The description text is in a separate text block that is positioned very close to the large text block.

2 **Click the word *Faust* with the Pointer tool to select this text block. Choose View > Fit Selection to zoom in on this element.**
You can quickly zoom in on any element on your page simply by selecting the element and choosing Fit Selection.

You cannot apply a gradient fill to type, although you can easily apply a gradient fill to a closed path. So what if you simply convert your text to paths?

3 With the text block still selected, choose Text > Convert to Paths or click the Convert to Paths button on the text toolbar.

This instantly changes the text characters into paths—just like the ones you create yourself with the Bezigon or Pen tool. The letters now appear selected as a group rather than a text block since you see only selection boxes at the corners, not a text block.

Note: Once text is converted to paths, you will not be able to edit it with the Text tool or change its characteristics with any of the text formatting controls. Make any changes to the text and apply desired font, type style, and other formatting options before you convert to paths.

4 Display the Fill Inspector. Change the fill type to gradient and use the menu at the bottom of the Inspector to change the ending color to a light yellow.

All of the character paths are now filled with the gradient.

Change to light yellow here

Once these characters are paths, you can also modify the paths to change the character shapes.

5 Click the Ungroup button on the toolbar or choose Modify > Ungroup.

The five individual paths are now visible. To easily work with these paths, without accidentally selecting the elements in the background, you will turn off the Preview mode.

Tip: The Keyline mode can be very useful in situations like this one, when you're working with overlapping shapes. In addition, FreeHand can display objects more quickly in Keyline mode than in Preview mode, so when you're working with complex illustrations and layouts, the Keyline mode can save you time.

6 Choose View > Preview to turn off the Preview mode and switch to the Keyline mode.

The Keyline mode allows you to see all of the elements clearly, without the fills and strokes. Notice that the word *Keyline* now appears at the bottom of your document window—this is a menu you can use to choose between the Preview and Keyline modes.

Choose Keyline here

To modify a path, you must first select the points you wish to move.

7 Use the Pointer tool to surround all of the points in the bottom part of the first character. Then release the mouse button.

You will now be able to move all of these selected points downward, to lengthen the stem of this character.

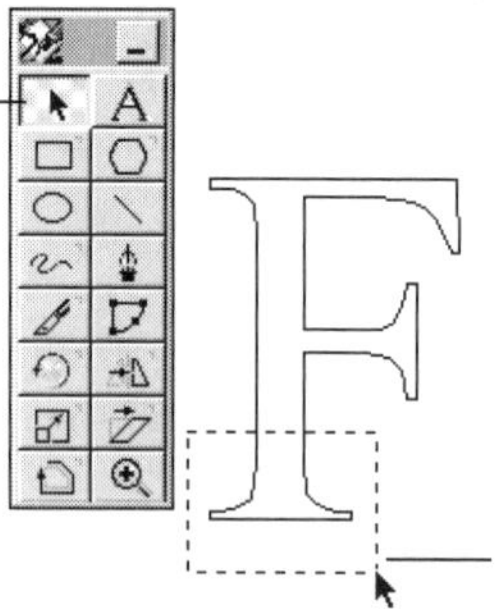

Pointer tool

Drag to surround points here

8 Point to one of the selected points and start to drag downward. Then press Shift to keep the movement vertical and not allow horizontal movement. Drag downward about half an inch and release the mouse button before you release the Shift key.

If you accidentally drag a control handle and distort the character shape, simply choose Edit > Undo and try again.

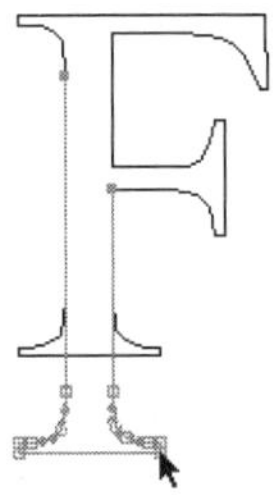

9 **Press Tab to deselect the element and turn the Preview mode back on to see how the artwork looks.**
You can change the display mode using the menu at the bottom of the screen or by choosing View > Preview.

Next you will make a change to the other four characters in this word.

10 **Select the second character and then hold Shift and click to add the third, fourth, and fifth characters in this word.**
All of the characters in *Faust* should be selected except the *F*.

11 **Choose Xtras > Distort > Envelope.**
Xtras are plug-in software extensions that enhance FreeHand's capabilities. Each Xtra adds a specific feature or group of features.

The Envelope Xtra displays a preview of the selected elements, surrounded by a path. This path is called an **envelope**. By adjusting the shape of this path, you can alter the outer shape of the selected elements.

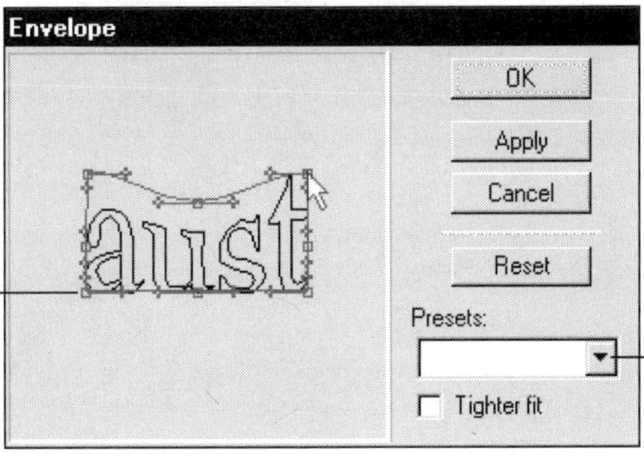

12 Drag the top corner points of the envelope path upward.

As you make changes to the envelope, the preview window shows what the character shapes will be.

13 When you are satisfied with the shape of the envelope, click OK.

The changes are applied to the selected elements.

14 Press Tab to deselect all elements and choose View > Fit To Page to see your completed artwork.

You have completed this lesson and are ready to return to the tutorial.

15 Choose File > Exit (Windows) or File > Quit (Macintosh).

If you opened this lesson file from within the interactive tutorial, you will be returned to the tutorial automatically. Otherwise, you can return to the tutorial by double-clicking the Instruct icon on the CD.

5 Creating Complex Layouts

This section consists of six lessons:

- Importing Artwork and Text into a Layout
- Using a Tracing Pattern
- Creating a Blend and Using Layers
- Creating a Clipping Path
- Joining a Blend to a Path
- Using Graphic Search and Replace

FreeHand provides many advanced features that enable you to produce your own rich illustrations and precise layouts. In this section you will import graphic and text files and control the way these elements interact on a page. You will also combine elements in new ways by blending shapes together, creating shapes that hide portions of other elements, and joining elements to one another. In the last lesson in this section you will explore the power of FreeHand's search and replace capability for graphics—a real time-saver if you ever need to make changes in your artwork.

Lesson 5-1

Importing Artwork and Text into a Layout

You can easily import text and graphics created in other programs into your layouts. In this lesson, you will import a text file and a graphic and see how to control the relationship between the two on a page.

1 **If the practice lesson 5-1 isn't open, go to the Lessons folder on the CD and open the file named 5-1.fh7.**
Several elements are already positioned on this page. You are ready to import the text.

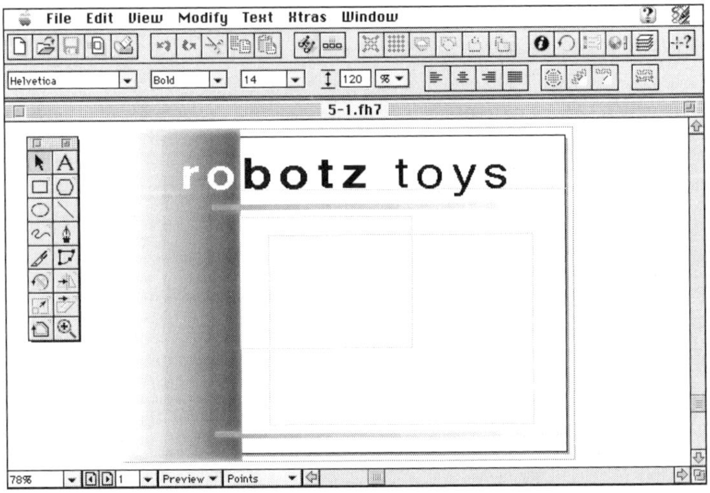

2 **Choose File > Import. Select the text file named 5-1.rtf located in the Lessons folder and click the Open button.**
This is a rich text format document (RTF), which contains formatted text from a word processor. When you click the Open button, you return to the document window with an import cursor displayed on the screen. You will use this cursor to position the imported element on the page.

3 **Position the import cursor at the upper-left corner of the large rectangular guide on this page. Drag down to the bottom-right corner of this guide and release the mouse.**

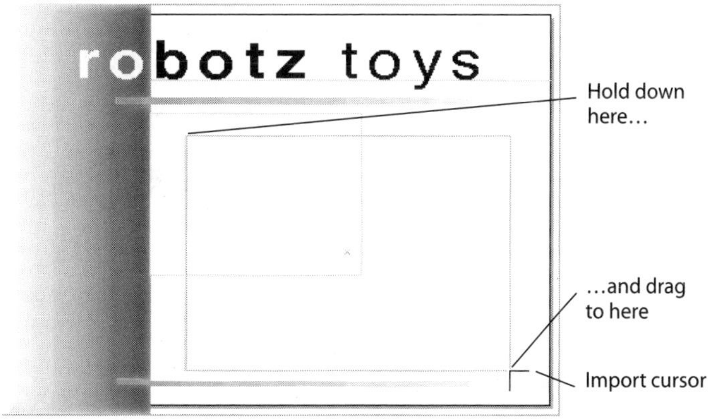

The text flows into the text block you just created by dragging with the import cursor. If your text block does not match the rectangular guide, you can use the Pointer tool to adjust its size or position by dragging the corner selection boxes of the text block.

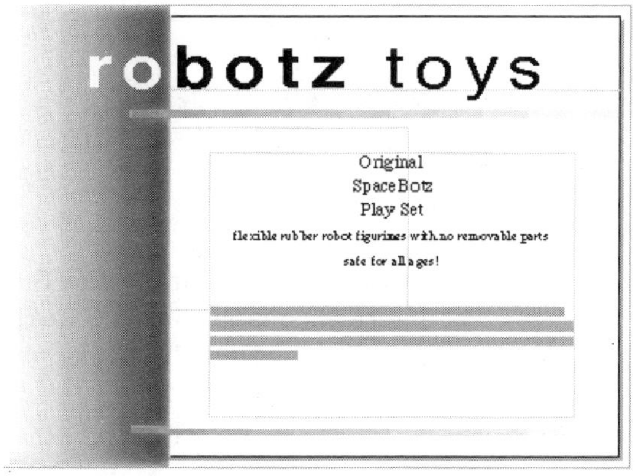

Next you will import an image and position it where the smaller rectangular guide indicates. However, to see all of the guide, you will need to move it in front of the graphics on the page by using the Layers panel.

4 **Display the Layers panel by choosing Window > Panels > Layers or by clicking its button on the toolbar.**

All nonprinting guides are located on the layer named Guides, which is currently below the Foreground layer in the Layers panel.

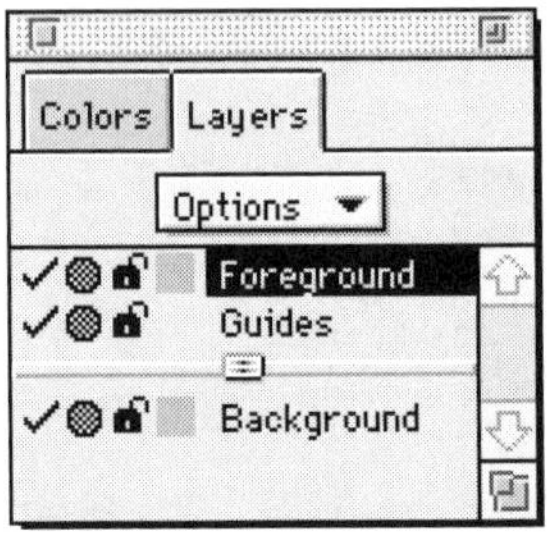

5 **Point to the name of the Guides layer in the Layers panel and drag it upward. Release the mouse button when the Guides layer is above the Foreground layer.**

The guides are now in front of the artwork on the page, so you can see where to position the graphic.

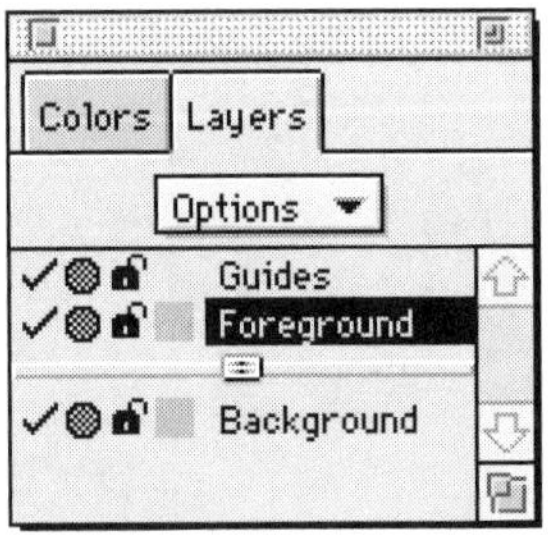

6 **Choose File > Import or click the Import button on the toolbar. Select the image named 5-1.tif located in the Lessons folder and click the Open button or press Enter (Windows) or Return (Macintosh).**

This image was created in Extreme 3D and modified in xRes, two of the other FreeHand Graphics Studio applications.

7 **Position the import cursor at the top-left corner of the smaller rectangular guide and click the mouse.**

The image appears on the page, but unfortunately it is overlapping the text. To solve this problem, you will use the **Run Around** feature to automatically wrap the text around this graphic.

Tip: Don't drag the import cursor when importing graphics or you will resize the image. Clicking the import cursor on the page imports the graphic in its original size and proportions.

8 With the image still selected, choose Text > Run Around Selection. Click the right button at the top of the dialog box to activate Run Around.

A dialog box appears where you can turn Run Around on or off and specify how much space you want between the graphic and the text on all four sides. In this case, the image overlaps the text only on the bottom right, so you will need to enter values for only those two positions.

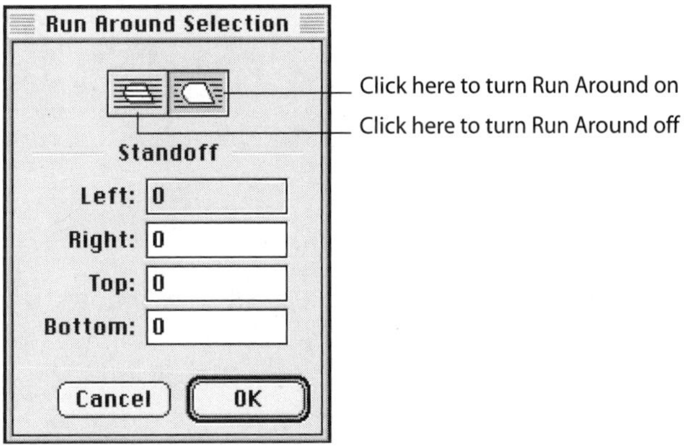

9 Change the value for the right and bottom edges to 9 points by entering *9* into each of these fields. Then click OK.

The text automatically wraps around the graphic, leaving the desired space along the bottom and right edges of the image.

The value is entered in points in this example because the measurements units are set to points for this document, as indicated by the Measurement Units menu at the bottom of the document window.

10 Press Tab to deselect the artwork so you can see your finished layout.

Tab can be used to deselect all elements, except when you are working with the Text tool or are in the process of entering values into panels and have not pressed Enter (Windows) or Return (Macintosh) to complete that operation.

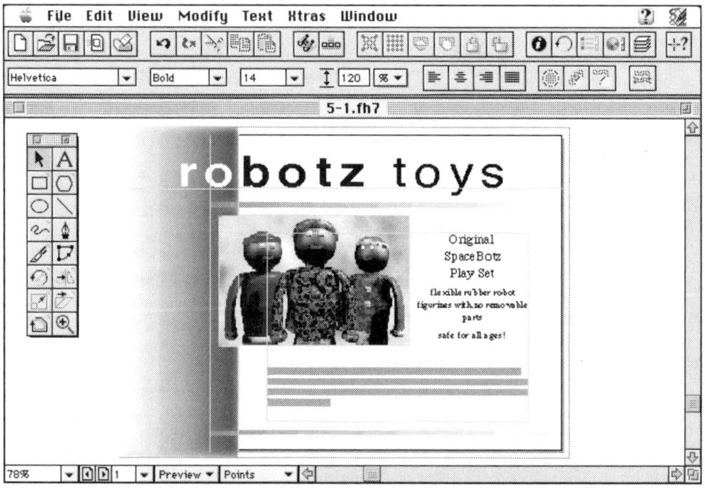

You have completed this lesson and are ready to return to the tutorial.

11 Choose File > Exit (Windows) or File > Quit (Macintosh).

If you opened this lesson file from within the interactive tutorial, you will be returned to the tutorial automatically. Otherwise, you can return to the tutorial by double-clicking the Instruct icon on the CD.

Lesson 5-2

Using a Tracing Pattern

A good way to accurately create paths and elements is to trace an existing image of the desired layout or artwork. For example, you can use a scanned image of a pencil sketch or other printed source as a pattern for tracing in FreeHand.

In this lesson you will import an xRes image to use as a tracing pattern for the artwork you will be creating. So you can use it as a tracing pattern, you will move it into the background layer, where it will be visible for tracing but will not print.

To trace this artwork, you can use the Bezigon or Pen tool to manually create paths that follow the shapes in the background image. You can also use the **Trace tool** to automatically create these elements, which is what you will do here.

1 **If the practice lesson 5-2 isn't open, go to the Lessons folder on the CD and open the file named 5-2.fh7.**
  This document contains one empty letter-size page.

2 **Click the Import button on the toolbar or choose File > Import. Select the image named 5-2.tif located in the Lessons folder on the CD and click the Open button.**

3 **Position the import cursor on the page and click the mouse.**
  An image of three wavy shapes appears on the page.

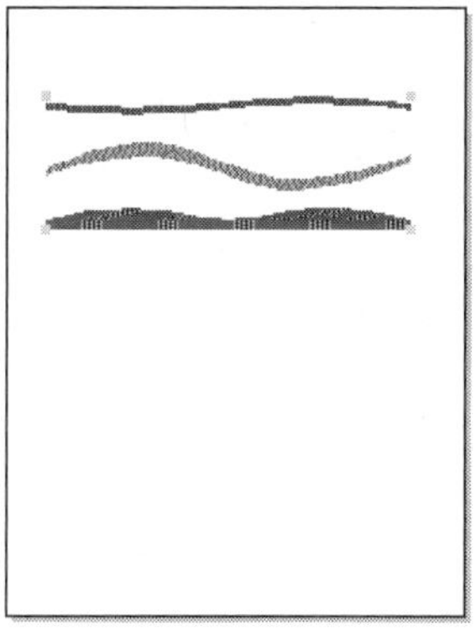

Tip: When you click the import cursor on the page, the top-left corner of the image will be positioned precisely where the import cursor was clicked. Since you may not know precisely where the image should be until you can see it on the page, simply click the import cursor somewhere in the document window and then use the Pointer tool to move the element into the desired position.

4 **If the graphic is not positioned entirely on the page, move it using the Pointer tool. Then press Tab to deselect the artwork.**
The precise location of the artwork on the page is not important, but it will be easier to see if the entire graphic is on the page. Enlarging your view of the artwork will also make it easier to see.

5 **Using the Zoom tool, position the cursor slightly above and to the left of the wavy shapes image and drag to surround the image with the magnification marquee. Then release the mouse.**
This enlarges your view of the area you surrounded so that it now fills the document window.

Next you will move the wavy shapes image to the background layer so you can use it as a tracing pattern.

6 **Display the Layers panel by clicking its button on the toolbar or by choosing Window > Panels > Layers.**

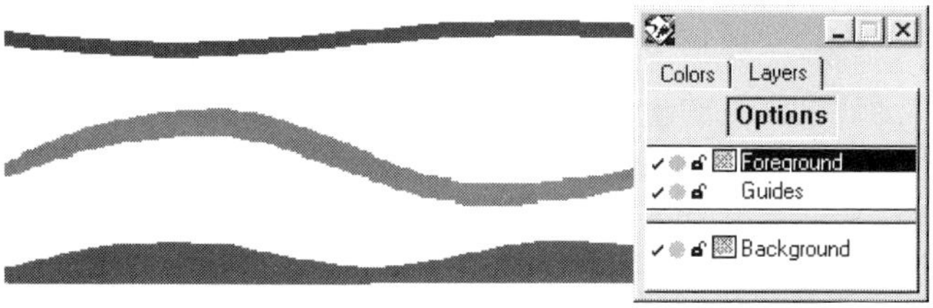

You can use layers to organize the artwork in your documents.

Note: Guides is a special layer that contains all nonprinting guides you may add to your page to help you position elements.

Any layer (except for Guides) that appears in the top portion of the Layers panel will print unless you tell it not to. These are called **foreground** layers. Layers that appear in the lower portion of the Layers panel are called **background** layers and do not print. The artwork on background layers appears dimmed on the screen

The layer named Foreground in this document is the default foreground layer in all FreeHand documents; Background is the default background layer. You will see in Lesson 5-3 how you can rename layers and use additional layers to help organize elements in your documents.

Now you are ready to move the imported image on the page to the Background layer.

7 Select the wavy shapes image with the Pointer tool and click Background in the Layers panel.

The artwork dims to indicate that it was moved to the background. The Background layer is also selected in the Layers panel, indicating that the selected item is located in that layer.

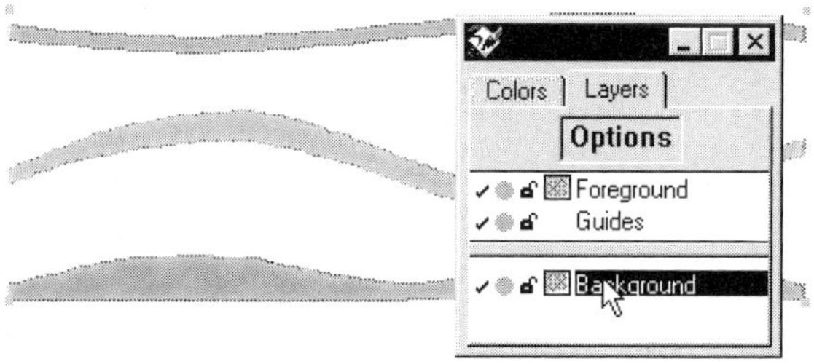

8 Click the Lock icon next to Background in the Layers panel to lock this layer.

Locking ensures that the pattern is not accidentally changed. It also makes the Foreground layer active—this is where you will create your artwork.

To hide the elements on a particular layer, click the check mark at the left of the layer name which indicates that a layer if visible. If the check mark is not displayed for an individual layer, the elements on that layer are hidden. To show elements on hidden layer, click the empty spot where the check mark was. In this case, you want to see all of the layers so you can trace the shapes in the background image, so you want a check mark to appear next to all the layer names.

Click here to lock

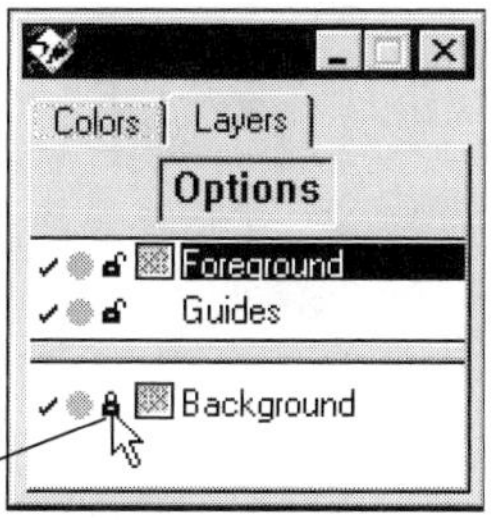

9 Close the Layers panel.

You are ready to begin tracing the background shapes. Instead of manually creating paths that match these shapes, you will use the Trace tool.

10 **Double-click the Trace tool in the toolbox to display Preference settings for this tool.**

You need to specify the settings before using the tool to control the way this tool will trace the image.

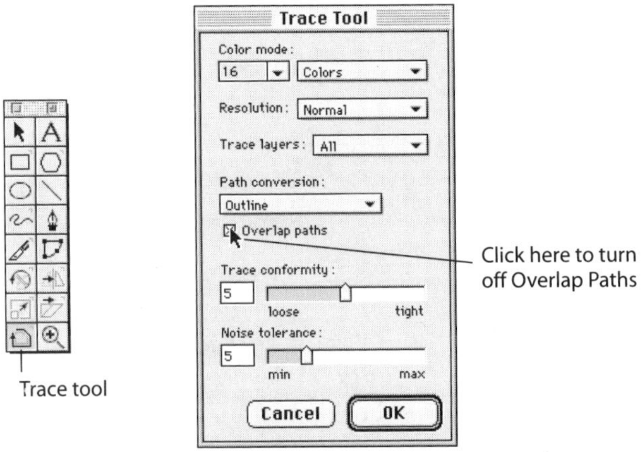

11 **Turn off Overlap Paths and click OK.**

You want these three shapes to be traced as three separate paths that don't touch one another.

12 **Position the Trace tool cursor above and to the left of the top shape, drag to surround all three shapes in the tracing pattern, and then release the mouse.**

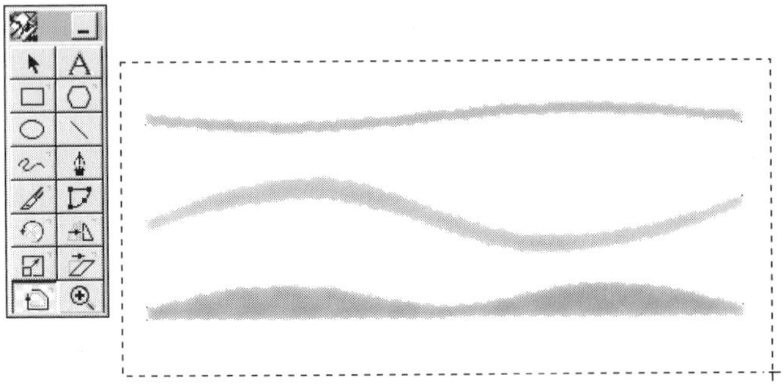

FreeHand automatically traces the shapes and applies the colors. Now you have three paths you can work with.

Experiment with the Trace tool and compare it to the results you get with the Pen or Bezigon tools. Although the Trace tool is quick and easy on simple shapes like the ones in this example, it does not always deliver the results you need for precise control over the paths.

You have completed this lesson and are ready to return to the tutorial.

13 Choose File > Exit (Windows) or File > Quit (Macintosh).
If you opened this lesson file from within the interactive tutorial, you will be returned to the tutorial automatically. Otherwise, you can return to the tutorial by double-clicking the Instruct icon on the CD.

Lesson 5-3

Creating a Blend and Using Layers

In this lesson you will first **blend** individual paths together, creating a smooth transition between the original shapes and colors. Then you will add this blend to another document to complete an illustration. Organizing your artwork by placing elements on different layers can simplify the process of selecting and modifying those elements later.

1 **If the practice lesson 5-3 isn't open, go to the Lessons folder on the CD and open the file named 5-3.fh7.**
This document contains three wavy shapes, like the ones you created in Lesson 5-2. In order to blend these elements together, they must first be selected.

2 **Select all three of the paths in this document with the Pointer tool by clicking one of the paths, holding down Shift, and clicking each of the other two paths.**
By holding down Shift you can add elements to the selection.

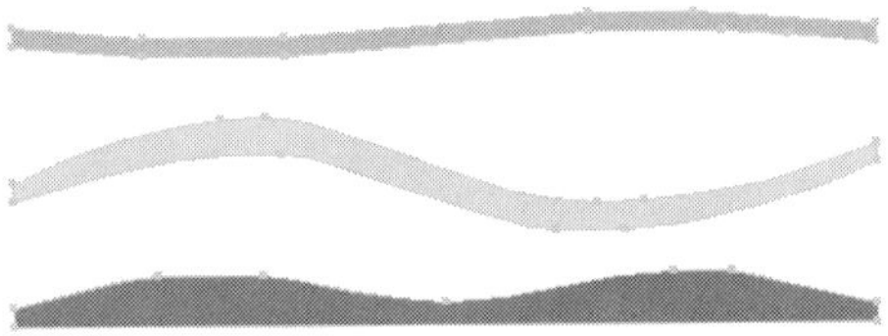

3 **Choose Modify >Combine > Blend.**
FreeHand creates intermediate shapes between the original paths and groups the entire blend together.

4 **Display the Object Inspector by clicking its button on the toolbar or choosing Window > Inspectors > Object.**

The Object Inspector displays the number of intermediate steps (or shapes) the selected blend contains.

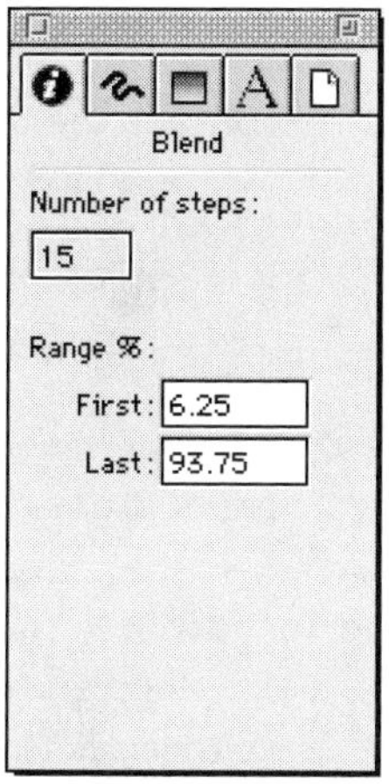

5 **Reduce the number of steps in the blend by entering *3* in the Number of Steps field and pressing Enter (Windows) or Return (Macintosh).**

Now you can clearly see the individual shapes created by the blend. Notice that the blend transforms both the shape and color of the objects.

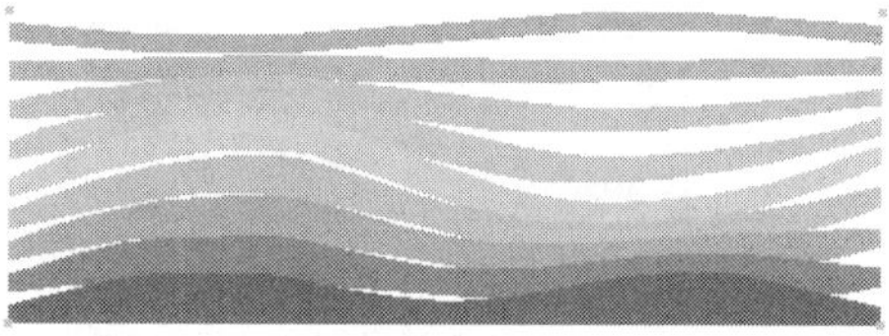

6 **Increase the number of steps in this blend to 25.**

This adds more intermediate shapes and colors for a smoother blend.

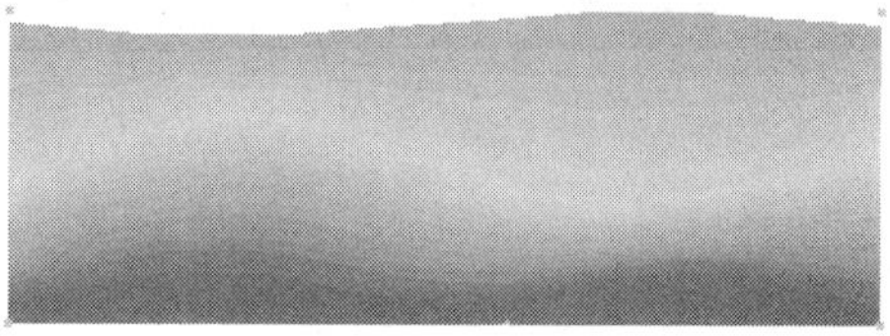

Now you're ready to use this blend in another FreeHand document.

7 **With the blend selected, choose Edit > Copy.**
Now that you have copied the artwork, open the illustration where you will paste the blend.

8 **Choose File > Open or click the Open button on the toolbar. Select the document named Beacon in the Lessons folder and click the Open button.**
The elements in this illustration are located on several separate layers. This organization will make selecting elements or making changes.

9 **Display the Layers panel to see the layers in this document.**
Notice that there are several foreground layers in this document (the ones in the top portion of the Layers panel). However, none of these layers is named Foreground. Evidently, the default layer with that name was either deleted or renamed as the illustration was constructed. That's not a problem, though—the layer names have no affect on your document. All of the layers in the top portion of this panel are foreground layers, and the artwork on these layers will print.

10 **Hide the Lighthouse layer by clicking the check mark next to the layer name in the Layers panel.**
The check mark disappears—and so does the lighthouse artwork because it is located on the hidden layer.

11 **Display the Lighthouse layer again by clicking at the far left of the layer name in the Layers panel.**
The check mark appears to indicate that the layer is visible again. Now you are ready to paste in the blend you created.

12 **Click the Paste button on the toolbar or choose Edit > Paste to add your blend to this document.**
The blend will be the water in this illustration. Notice that a layer named Foreground was added to the Layers panel. When you created this blend in the other document, the artwork was in a layer named Foreground. When you copy and paste, the artwork is pasted onto a layer with the same name. Since no layer named Foreground existed in this document, FreeHand automatically created one!

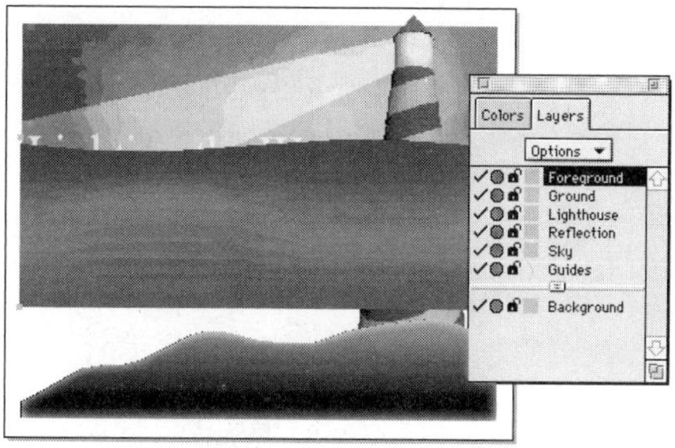

13 **Rename the Foreground layer by double-clicking its name in the Layers panel, entering *Water* as the new name, and pressing Enter (Windows) or Return (Macintosh).**

14 **Move the blend into position so that it covers the gap between the sky and the ground in the illustration.**

Now the only problem with the water is that it looks like a flood!

15 **Drag the Water layer down in the Layers panel and position it beneath the Reflection layer.**

As you can see, these separate layers make it easy to reorganize the elements in your document.

16 **Press Tab to deselect all of the elements in this document.**

Always make sure that no elements are selected before clicking a different layer name to make that layer active. Clicking a layer name with an item selected will move that item to the layer you clicked.

Tip: When working with layers, make sure that you do not click a layer name when an element is selected unless you intentionally want to move the selected element to a different layer.

17 **Click the Reflection layer to make this layer active.**

New elements are always created in the active layer.

18 **Hide all of the foreground layers except Reflection by clicking the check marks next to their names.**

This will allow you to clearly see the artwork on the Reflection layer.

There are two ellipses on this layer. One of these is filled with a very light shade, so you may not even see it on the page.

19 **Choose Edit > Select > All to select the two elements on this layer.**

Select All will select all elements on the page, but elements on hidden or locked layers cannot be selected. Since you hid all of the other layers, the only elements remaining were the two on the Reflection layer.

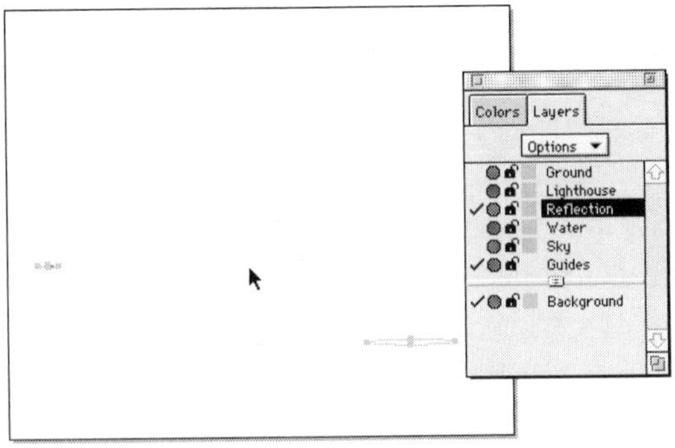

20 Create a blend between the two ellipses by choosing Modify > Combine > Blend.

FreeHand creates intermediate shapes that progressively change in color and size between the original two elements.

21 Reduce the number of steps in this blend to 15 using the Object Inspector.

Remember to press Enter (Windows) or Return (Macintosh) to apply the change.

Now make sure that nothing is selected before you display the hidden layers again.

22 Deselect the artwork by pressing Tab.

23 Display all of the layers again by clicking along the far left edge of the Layers panel next to the layer names.

You have completed this lesson and are ready to return to the tutorial.

24 Choose File > Exit (Windows) or File > Quit (Macintosh).

If you opened this lesson file from within the interactive tutorial, you will be returned to the tutorial automatically. Otherwise, you can return to the tutorial by double-clicking the Instruct icon on the CD.

Lesson 5-4

Creating a Clipping Path

In this lesson you will see how you can trim artwork to fit inside another path.

1 **If the practice lesson 5-4 isn't open, go to the Lessons folder on the CD and open the file named 5-4.fh7.**
The sun, sunbeams, and hills in this document are grouped together. You want to trim this group of elements to fit perfectly inside the sky rectangle currently behind this group on the page.

2 **Drag the sunbeam group—the sun, sunbeams, and hills—with the Pointer tool and position it in front of the sky.**
The sunbeam group should overlap the sky.

Cut button

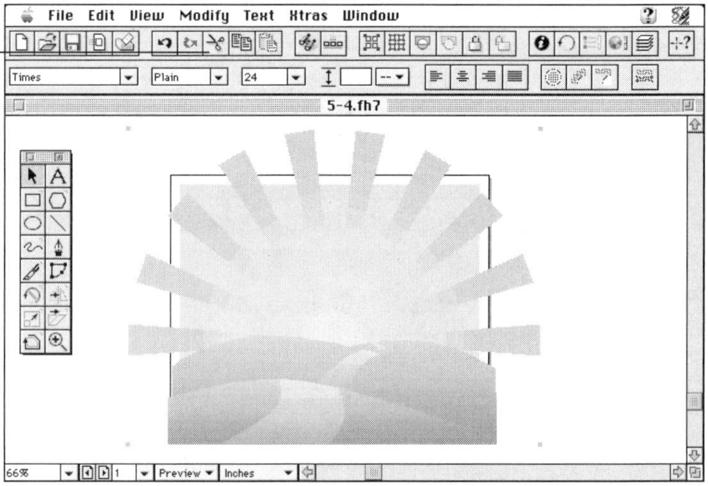

3 **Choose Edit > Cut or click the Cut button on the toolbar.**
The sunbeams disappear from the page—but only temporarily.

4 **Select the sky rectangle and choose Edit > Paste Inside.**
The sunbeam artwork appears inside the rectangle. This rectangle is now called a **clipping path**, because it clips off the portions of the graphics that don't fit inside it.

5 **Choose View > Fit To Page to see your work more clearly.**
The rectangle should still be selected.

6 **Drag the handle displayed inside the selected clipping path to reposition the sunbeam group within the sky rectangle.**
You can move the contents of a clipping path using this handle, which appears whenever a clipping path is selected.

7 **Press Tab to deselect everything.**
The handle disappears when the clipping path is no longer selected.

8 **To remove the contents of the clipping path, select the clipping path with the Pointer tool. Then choose Edit > Cut Contents.**
The contents of the clipping path are now pasted in front of the path. They are no longer affected by the path in any way.

9 **Click the Undo button on the toolbar or choose Edit > Undo to restore the sunbeam group to its position inside the rectangle.**
FreeHand supports multiple levels of undo, so if Undo did not return your document to this stage, you can choose Undo one or more additional times.

10 **Press Tab to deselect everything.**
You have completed this lesson and are ready to return to the tutorial.

11 **Choose File > Exit (Windows) or File > Quit (Macintosh).**
If you opened this lesson file from within the interactive tutorial, you will be returned to the tutorial automatically. Otherwise, you can return to the tutorial by double-clicking the Instruct icon on the CD.

Lesson 5-5

Joining a Blend to a Path

Now you will create a blend between several elements and then wrap the blend around a page as a border by joining it to a path.

1 **If the practice lesson 5-5 isn't open, go to the Lessons folder on the CD and open the file named 5-5.fh7.**
This document contains a sunset illustration, like the one you created in Lesson 5-4. Four squares are located on the pasteboard below the page.

2 **Draw a rectangle that matches the guide displayed along the outside edges of the page.**
This rectangle is the element to which you will attach a blend. The rectangle is filled with white, which covers the artwork on this page. The fill and stroke of this element will disappear when you attach the blend.

3 **Position the Pointer tool on a blank area above and to the left of the four squares on the pasteboard below the page. Select these elements by dragging to surround all four squares and then releasing the mouse.**

You can also click one of the squares with the Pointer tool, hold down Shift, and click each of the remaining squares to select all four at once.

4 **Choose Modify > Combine > Blend.**

This menu choice automatically creates intermediate shapes between each of the four original elements.

5 **With the blend still selected, hold down Shift and click the large rectangle around the outside edge of the page to select it along with the blend.**

The blend and the path you want to join it to must both be selected.

6 Choose Modify > Combine > Join Blend To Path.

The blend now follows the rectangular path around the sunset artwork, and the fill and stroke of the rectangle have disappeared.

7 Display the Object Inspector and change the number of steps in this blend to 25. Then press Enter (Windows) or Return (Macintosh).

The blend now has many more elements, making it a more effective border for the illustration.

You have completed this lesson and are ready to return to the tutorial.

8 Choose File > Exit (Windows) or File > Quit (Macintosh).

If you opened this lesson file from within the interactive tutorial, you will be returned to the tutorial automatically. Otherwise, you can return to the tutorial by double-clicking the Instruct icon on the CD.

Lesson 5-6

Using Graphic Search and Replace

FreeHand's Graphic search and replace feature enables you to make changes to multiple graphics in your document without having to find, select, or change each element one by one.

1 **If the practice lesson 5-6 isn't open, go to the Lessons folder on the CD and open the file named 5-6.fh7.**
The border in the artwork here is a blend made up of individual elements containing tints of a single brown color. You will change these elements to the same tints of burgundy.

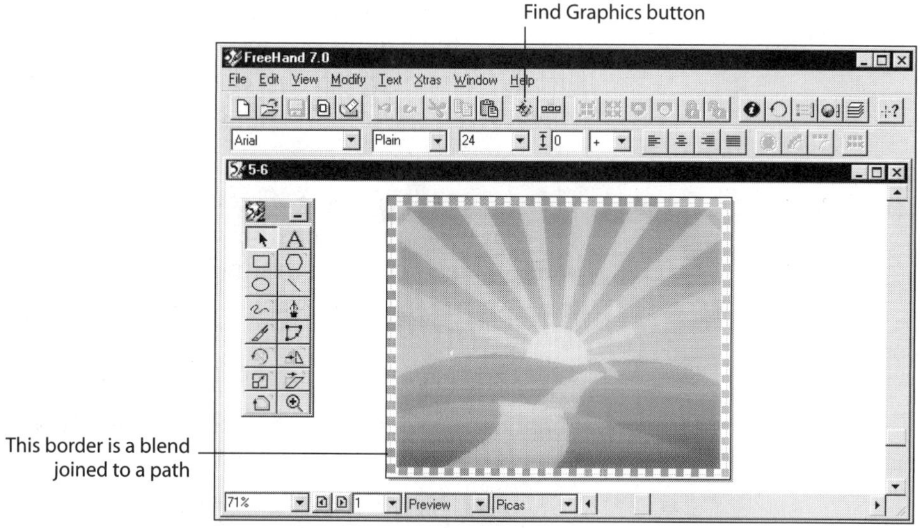

2 **Click the Find Graphics button on the toolbar or choose Edit > Find and Replace > Graphics.**

A new panel appears where you will specify what you are looking for and what changes you would like to make.

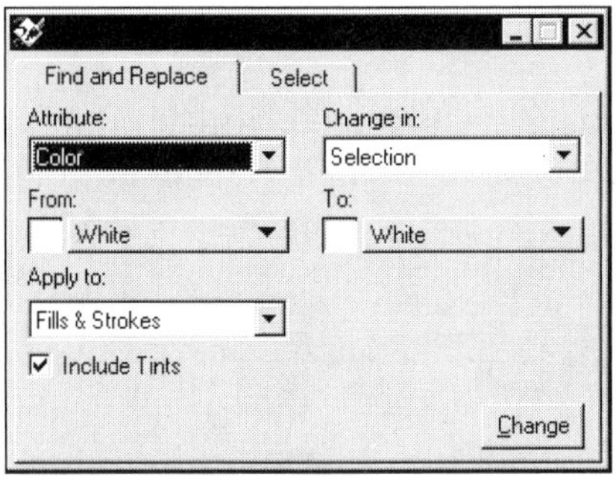

3 **In the Attribute menu, select Color, then select Brown in the From menu. Then in the Apply To menu, select Fills. Turn on Include Tints if it is not already on.**

Include Tints will ensure that all elements that contain any tint of brown in the fill will be selected.

4 **In the Change In menu, select Document.**

This changes all instances of brown throughout the document. The brown color is not used anywhere in this document except in the border, so this is the setting you want. There may be times when you will not want to make a change throughout the document. In those cases, you can first select the elements you want to search and then set the Change In menu to Selection.

5 **Change the color in the To field to Burgundy. Then click the Change button.**

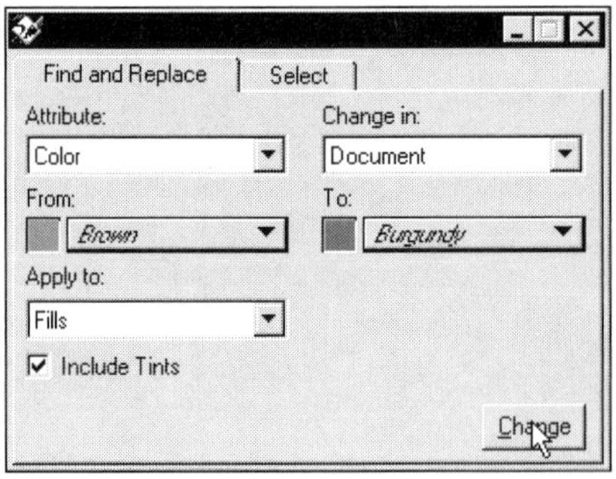

Burgundy now replaces the brown color throughout the document, and tints of burgundy now replace the same tints of brown.

FreeHand's ability to find and change graphics within documents will be very useful as you create and modify complex illustrations and layouts.

You have completed this lesson and are ready to return to the tutorial.

6 **Choose File > Exit (Windows) or File > Quit (Macintosh).**
If you opened this lesson file from within the interactive tutorial, you will be returned to the tutorial automatically. Otherwise, you can return to the tutorial by double-clicking the Instruct icon on the CD.

6 Printing and Exporting Artwork

This section consists of two lessons:

- Exporting Artwork for Use in Other Programs
- Printing a Document

Once you've completed your own illustrations in FreeHand, you can use the artwork in several ways—for instance, you can transfer the document to a different computer platform, work with the FreeHand artwork in other applications, and print the document at the highest quality your printer or output device can produce.

Lesson 6-1

Exporting Artwork for Use in Other Programs

FreeHand 7 files are the same on both the Macintosh and PC platforms, so no special preparation is needed to switch your files from one system to another. Simply save your file as you would normally, and you can open the file directly using FreeHand on either computer platform. Extreme 3D, the three-dimensional design application included in the FreeHand Graphics Studio, can also import native FreeHand files on both the Macintosh and Windows platforms. (You will import a FreeHand file into Extreme 3D in Section 7 of this tutorial.)

To use your FreeHand artwork in other applications, you need to use the Export command. In this lesson you will explore the various file formats that FreeHand can export and learn when they may be useful for your own projects.

1 **If the practice lesson 6-1 isn't open, go to the Lessons folder on the CD and open the file named 6-1.fh7.**
This file contains completed artwork ready for export to a different application.

2 **Choose File > Export.**
A dialog box appears where you can identify a location for the new file, enter a name for the file, and choose a file format.

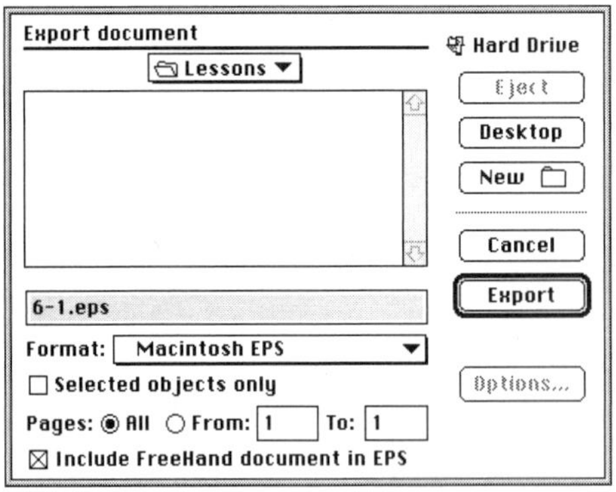

The default format for exporting FreeHand artwork is as an EPS, or Encapsulated PostScript, file. This is the best format to use for print production, because it delivers the same quality as the original FreeHand artwork. The EPS format also can be imported into the leading page layout applications, including QuarkXPress and Adobe PageMaker.

FreeHand provides EPS formats for both platforms, so you can easily prepare artwork for both computer systems.

3 **Hold down the mouse on the Format menu to display the wide range of file formats FreeHand exports.**
The formats available enable you to create files ready to use in your own print, multimedia, and Internet projects. FreeHand also supports several other formats so you can prepare artwork for other specific applications.

To save a file for a multimedia project, you select Formats > BMP (Windows) or Formats > PICT (Macintosh). To use your FreeHand files in multimedia applications such as Macromedia Director and Authorware, you select the bitmap format appropriate for the platform where you are developing the multimedia project.

To prepare a graphic for use on a Web page, you would choose Formats > GIF. You can also select JPEG and PNG. These three formats are the most popular bitmap formats for the World Wide Web.

Note: In Section 10 of this tutorial, you will explore Shockwave technology, which allows you to embed high-resolution FreeHand artwork in your Web pages as an alternative to the bitmap formats described here.

4 **Click Setup (Windows) or Options (Macintosh) to display specific controls for the file format you choose. Then click the More button to see other options, as well.**
Although these buttons are not available for every format, you will be able to choose your own settings for the graphics you create in formats that do offer choices. For example, many of the bitmap image formats give you control over the pixel resolution of the exported image. The GIF format, for instance, offers you the Transparent and Interlaced options when you're creating that type of graphic.

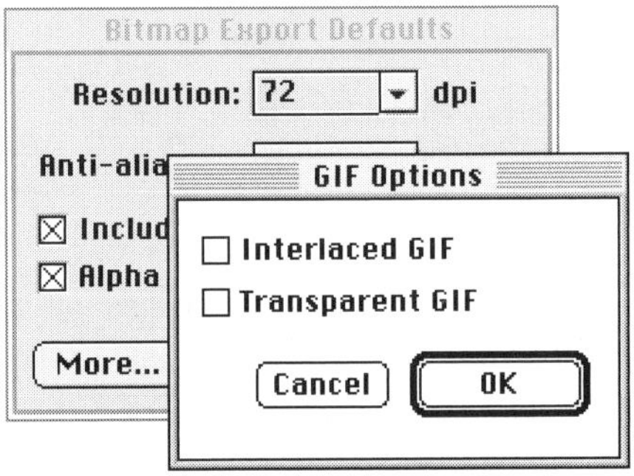

Several formats are available for preparing graphics for specific applications.

5 **Choose Formats > xRes LRG.**
This command prepares artwork for use in Macromedia xRes. Macromedia xRes is the digital painting and image editing application included in the FreeHand Graphics Studio. (You will explore the features of xRes in Section 8 of this tutorial.)

6 **Select Formats > Photoshop EPS.**
This command saves a version of your file ready to open in Adobe Photoshop.

The other application-specific formats available allow you to prepare artwork as files for previous versions of FreeHand, as Adobe Illustrator files, or as PDF files for viewing in Adobe Acrobat.

When you have selected the location, name, and file format you desire, you click the Export button to create a new file with these characteristics. In this lesson you can export a file if you want, but it is not necessary at this time.

7 **Click Cancel to return to the document window without exporting a file.**

As you can see, because FreeHand offers such a wide variety of export formats, it works equally well whether you're designing for print, multimedia, or the World Wide Web. It also enables you to use your artwork in all three of these types of projects simply by exporting the same artwork to different formats.

You have completed this lesson and are ready to return to the tutorial.

8 **Choose File > Exit (Windows) or File > Quit (Macintosh).**

If you opened this lesson file from within the interactive tutorial, you will be returned to the tutorial automatically. Otherwise, you can return to the tutorial by double-clicking the Instruct icon on the CD.

Lesson 6-2

Printing a Document

When you're ready to print your artwork, FreeHand enables you to control every aspect of the process. FreeHand creates PostScript artwork, which is resolution independent. That means that it will print at the highest resolution possible on any printer or output device that uses the PostScript page description language.

In this lesson, you will explore the controls available when printing to PostScript printers. If you don't have a PostScript printer, your Print dialog box will be different from the one shown in the tutorial and will display the options available for your specific printer. Some of the options described here may not be available on printers that do not use PostScript.

1 **If the practice lesson 6-2 isn't open, go to the Lessons folder on the CD and open the file named 6-2.fh7.**
This document contains a completed sunset illustration, ready to be printed.

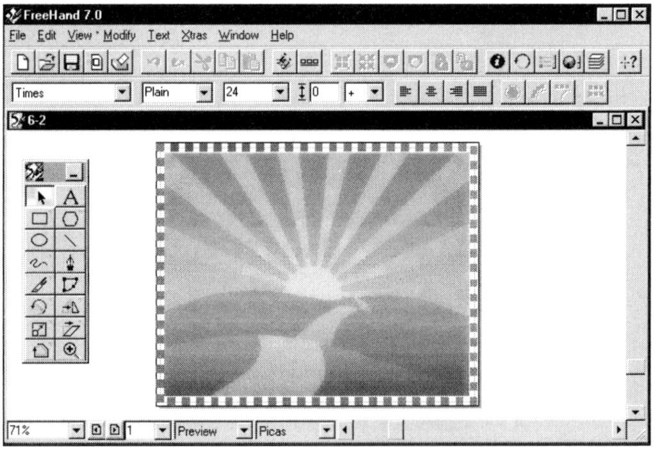

2 Choose File > Print.

The Print dialog box appears. At the top of this dialog box, you can set the number of copies and identify which pages to print (if your document contains multiple pages).

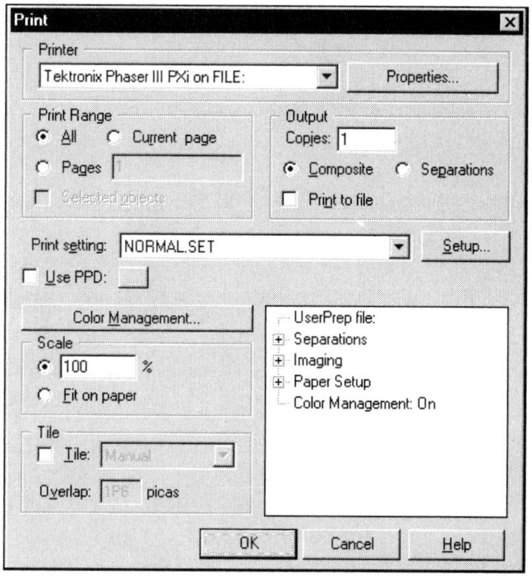

Clicking OK (Windows) or Print (Macintosh) now will print the document using the default settings. To add crop marks, change the paper size, or make other custom settings, you use FreeHand's Print Setup controls.

3 Click Setup to customize the settings.

You can apply these setting just to the current print job or use them for future jobs as well.

On the left side of the Print Setup dialog box, a preview window displays the document as it would print on the page with the current settings. On the right side of the dialog box, three tabbed panels let you control the printing process.

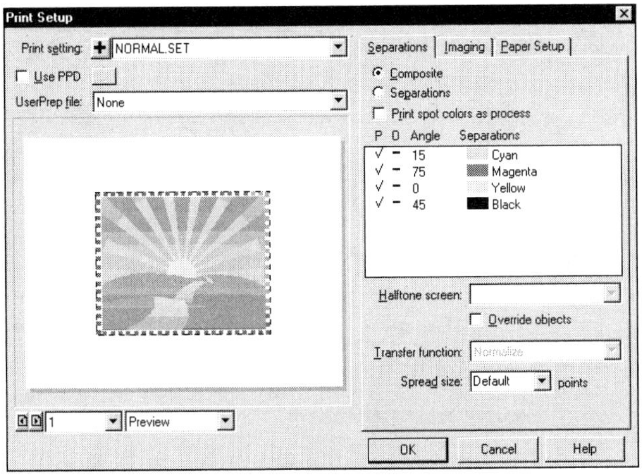

4 Click the Separations tab at the top right to display the controls for color output.

Here you can choose composite output or color separations.

5 Click the Imaging tab. Click File Name and Date to add a label and click Crop Marks to activate this feature.

The preview window displays the labels and crop marks as they will appear on the printed page.

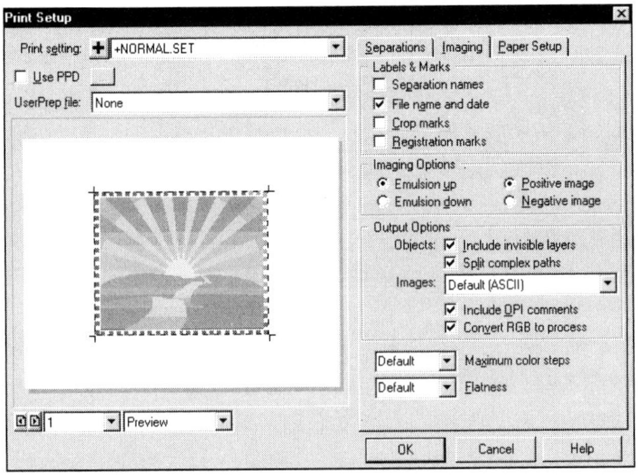

6 **Click the Paper Setup tab to display options for changing the paper size and orientation.**

The paper sizes offered depend upon the printer you are using. There may not be any paper size options available until after you identify a specific printer.

7 **At the top left of the Print Setup dialog box, click the Use PPD check box.**

An open dialog box appears where you can select a PostScript Printer Description file, or PPD.

Click here to choose PostScript Printer Description file

Then the Select PPD dialog box appears where you can select the PPD for your printer

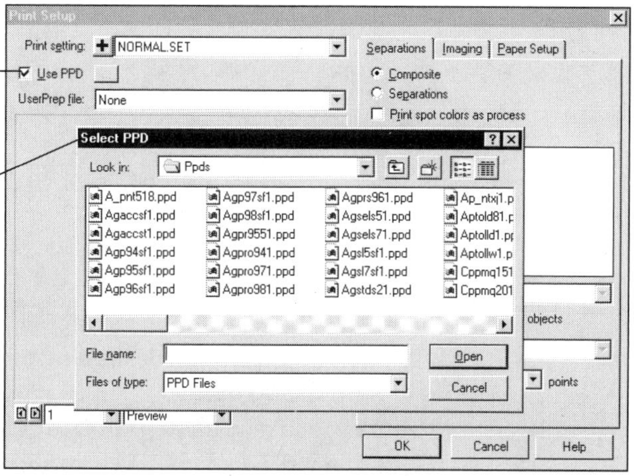

8 **Select your printer from the list and click Open.**

Once you've selected a PPD, the specific options available for your printer—such as the various paper sizes supported by this printer—appear as choices in the Print Setup box.

9 Change the paper size using the menu in the Paper Setup panel at the right, if it is available.

The preview window is automatically updated to reflect the new paper size. Different paper sizes may or may not be displayed, depending upon the PPD selected.

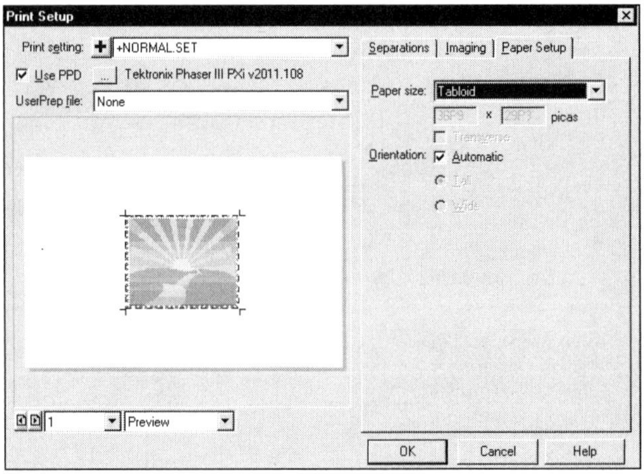

10 After selecting the desired settings, click OK to return to the Print dialog box.

Now you're ready to print! To print the artwork, you click OK (Windows) or Print (Macintosh).

11 Click the Cancel button to cancel the print request.

You do not need to actually print this illustration, unless you would like to see a printed version.

You have completed this lesson and are ready to return to the tutorial.

12 Choose File > Exit (Windows) or File > Quit (Macintosh).

If you opened this lesson file from within the interactive tutorial, you will be returned to the tutorial automatically. Otherwise, you can return to the tutorial by double-clicking the Instruct icon on the CD.

7 Creating 3D Images with Extreme 3D

Note: If you own a copy of Extreme 3D, you can use it to practice the lessons in this chapter, or you can work with the training version of Extreme 3D that is on the CD. (You do not need these programs to watch the tutorials, only to use the practice files.)

To run the training version of Extreme 3D, you need to install it on your hard drive. See the installation instructions in the introduction to this book. You will need at least 16 megabytes of RAM to run Extreme 3D (24 megabytes is recommended). If you're using a Macintosh, a Power PC is recommended; for Windows, a Pentium processor is recommended.

This section consists of two lessons:

- Getting Started with Extreme 3D
- Working with 3D Models

Extreme 3D, Macromedia's 3D illustration and animation application, is another member of the FreeHand Graphics Studio suite. It enables you to create three-dimensional artwork for your print, multimedia, and Web projects. You create three-dimensional elements, or **models**, by starting with two-dimensional shapes, called **profiles**. Next you arrange your models to compose a scene or create an animation. Then you adjust your view of the artwork and apply surface materials. The final step is to **render** the finished image, which creates a two-dimensional image from the three-dimensional geometry, lights, and materials.

Lesson 7-1

Getting Started with Extreme 3D

Note: You will need to install the training version of Extreme 3D from the CD to practice this lesson. Please read the special instructions on the first page of this section.

This lesson will help you get acquainted with the controls and capabilities of Extreme 3D.

1 **Go to the Lessons folder on the CD and open the file named 7-1.e3d.**

An Extreme 3D document window, called the **workspace**, opens. This is your window into the 3D **world**. The grid in the center of this window is called the **working plane**; it's part of an infinite grid that extends throughout the Extreme 3D world. Everything you draw or import is added to the world *on* the working plane.

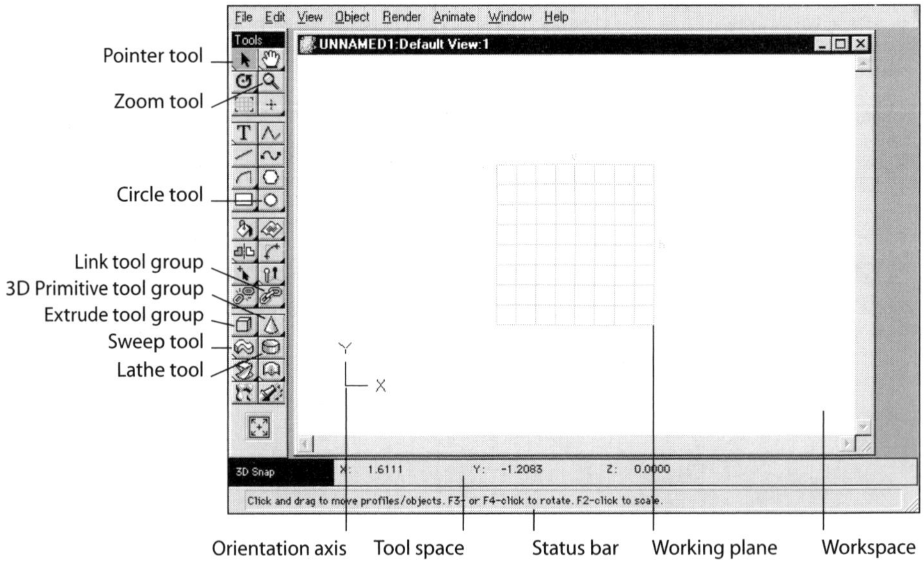

2 **Open the Object menu and make sure that Auto Working Plane to View is not checked. If it is checked, select it to turn it off.**

With this option off, the working plane will remain in the current orientation until you change it.

3 **Choose View > Three-Quarters.**
This enables you to clearly see the three dimensions you are working with. These dimensions are represented by the orientation axis in the lower-left corner of the workspace. X is the horizontal axis, Y is the vertical axis, and Z is the axis representing depth.

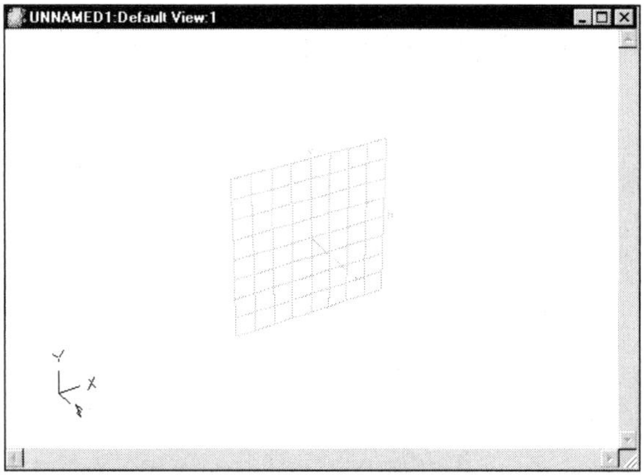

4 **Select the Circle tool in the toolbox.**
Notice the **status bar** at the bottom of your screen. This identifies the tool you're pointing to in the toolbox and indicates how to use that tool once you move it into the workspace.

5 **Drag to draw a circle anywhere in the workspace.**
You have just created a two-dimensional profile. This is a perfect circle but it doesn't look like one, since you are viewing it from an angle.

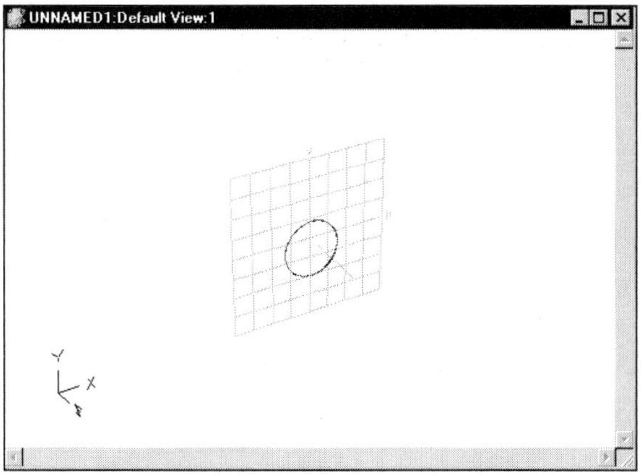

6 **Select the circular profile with the Pointer tool and drag it to the different corners of the workspace.**

As you drag, you move the profile in just two dimensions: horizontally and vertically along the working plane. (Remember that this plane extends beyond the edges of the visible portion, throughout the world.)

If you watch closely, the circle seems to shrink when you move it down and to the right. As you drag up and to the left, it appears to get larger. The circle actually never changes in size, but it appears to change size as you move it closer to you or farther away, just as it would in the real world. This is known as **perspective.**

You use two-dimensional profiles like this circle to create different kinds of three-dimensional objects.

7 **Choose Edit > Copy to make a copy of the circle so you can use it later.**

8 **Choose the Extrude tool in the toolbox. With the circle still selected, draw a line in the workspace in any direction approximately 1½ inches long.**

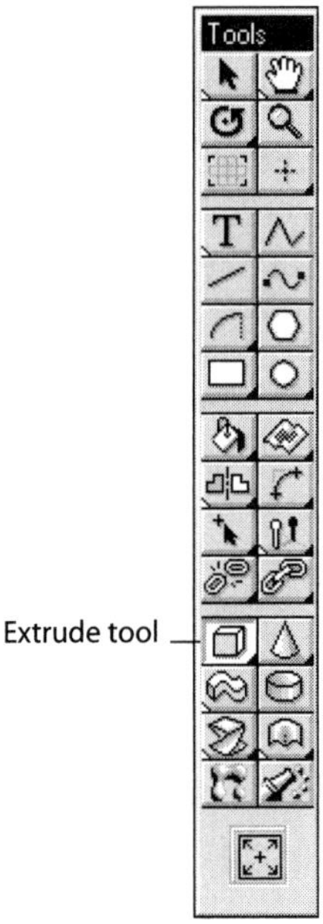

When you release the mouse, a cylinder appears. This 3D object—an **extrusion**—was formed by pulling out the circular profile the length of the line you drew with the Extrude tool.

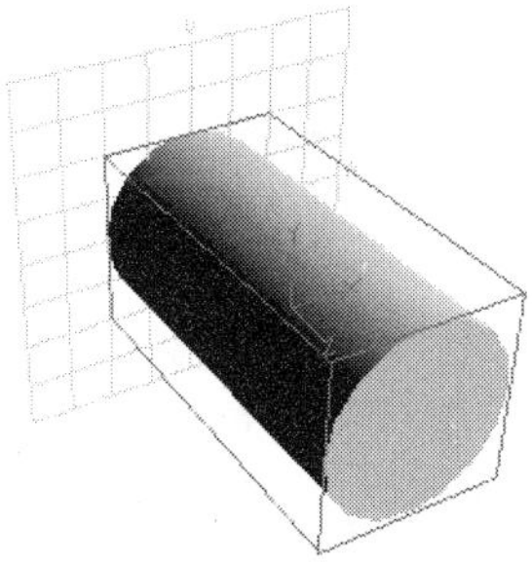

9 **With the Pointer tool, move this cylinder to the lower-right corner of the workspace.**
Notice that the status bar displays **modifier keys** you can hold down while dragging with the Pointer tool. These allow you to scale or rotate the element as you drag.

10 **Hold down F2 (Windows) or Control (Macintosh) and drag the mouse upward or downward in the workspace to make the element larger or smaller.**

11 **Hold down F3 or F4 (Windows) or Option or Command (Macintosh) and drag with the Pointer tool to rotate the object.**
You can use the keys individually or together to control the way the element rotates. With a bit of practice, you will find that these modifier keys enable you to both scale and rotate objects quickly and easily, without having to change tools.

Tip: Always deselect elements before pasting others. Otherwise, the element you paste will replace the object that is selected in the workspace.

12 **Click an empty part of the workspace to deselect the cylinder.**
Next you will paste another copy of the circle into the workspace.

13 **Choose Edit > Paste to put another copy of the circle in the workspace so you can create another 3D object.**
The pasted circle appears centered on the working plane.

14 **Select the Lathe tool. Make sure that 360 degrees is the angle entered into the tool space near the bottom of the screen, just above the status bar.**

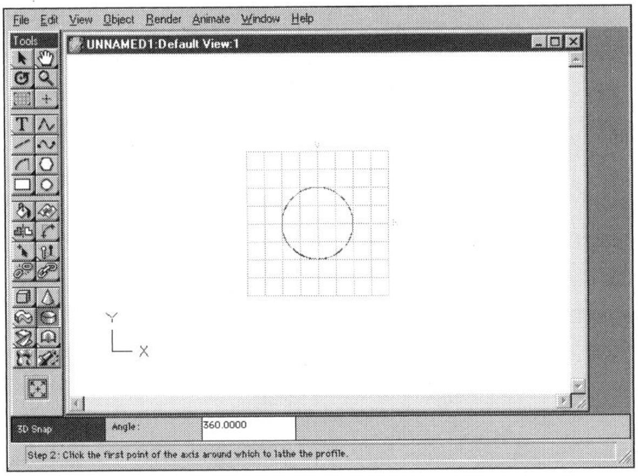

Entering values in the tool space controls the way a tool is applied. Instead of pulling a profile out along a straight line like the Extrude tool, the Lathe tool rotates a profile around an axis. Specifying an angle of 360 degrees ensures that the profile will rotate all of the way around the axis and connect to itself.

15 Click the circle once to select it and then draw a vertical line along the left edge of the working plane to define a rotation axis.
The circle revolves 360 degrees around the line you drew, creating a shape that resembles a bagel.

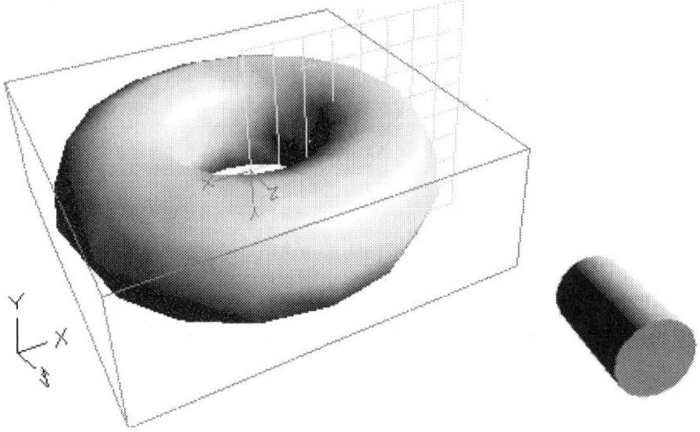

16 Using the Pointer tool, double-click this 3D object.
This opens the object so you can edit the original profile.

17 Drag the point along the outer edge of the circular profile that appears within this opened object to make the circle larger or smaller.

Changing the profile automatically changes the 3D element based on that profile. As you can see, you can easily make changes to the objects you create.

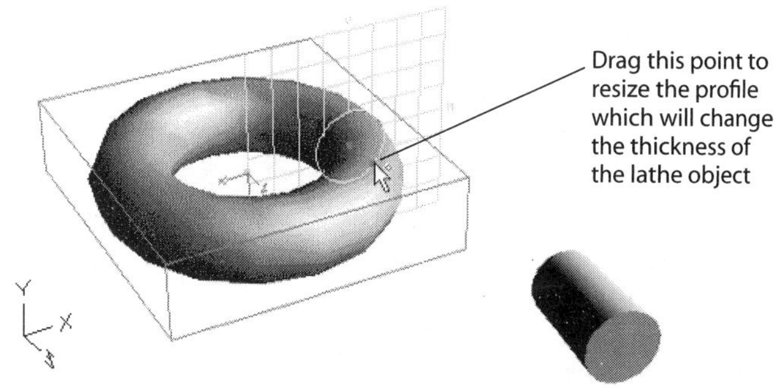

18 Choose the Polygon tool in the toolbox. In the tool space, change the number of sides to *5*.

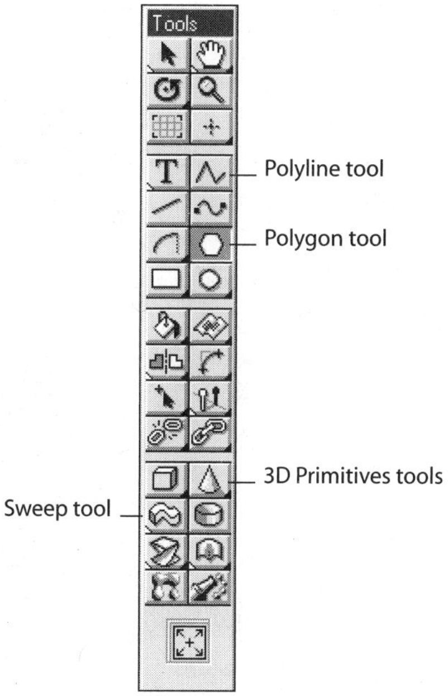

The tool space allows you to define the number of sides this polygon will have before you draw the profile.

19 Click and drag to create a small polygon anywhere in the workspace.

The polygon you create is a pentagon, because you specified 5 sides in the tool space before you drew the profile. You will **sweep** this profile along a path to create another type of three-dimensional object. To create the path, you will use the Polyline tool, which works like a connect-the-dots game. The path will be a Z-shaped line.

20 Create a Z-shaped line by clicking the Polyline tool once to start a line, moving to a new position and clicking again, and then moving to another new position and clicking once more.

This line will be the path you will sweep the polygon profile along.

21 Choose the Sweep tool from the toolbox.

A swept object is similar to an extrusion, except that the profile is pulled along any selected path, rather than just in one direction.

22 As the status bar instructs, click once on the pentagon profile you created with the Polygon tool. Then click once on the sweep path (the line you created with the Polyline tool).

The pentagon is swept along the path.

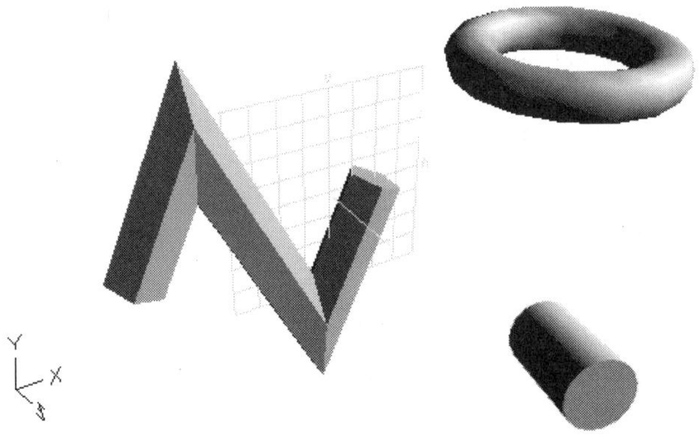

Extrusion, lathe, and sweep objects are just three examples of the different types of 3D objects you can create in Extreme 3D.

You can also create 3D elements directly, without creating a two-dimensional profile, using one of the 3D Primitive tools.

23 Select the Sphere tool by holding down the mouse button on the 3D Primitives tool group and moving the mouse slightly to pop up the other tools in this group.

Tools that have a black mark in the bottom-right corner are members of **tool groups** that pop up when you hold down the mouse button and move the cursor over them.

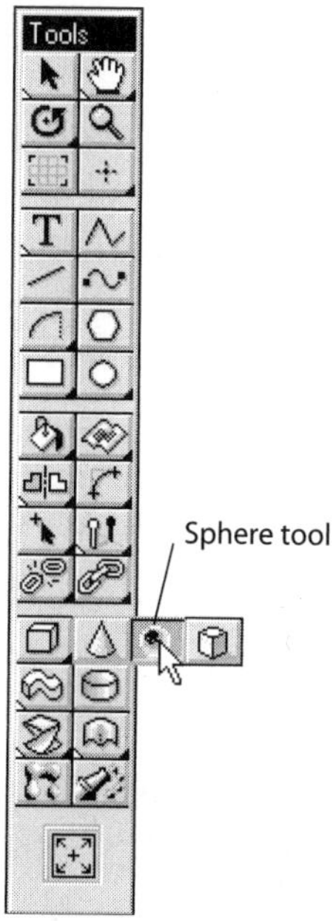

24 Position the cursor anywhere in the workspace and drag to draw a three-dimensional sphere in one step.

As you can see, Extreme 3D makes it easy to construct a variety of 3D objects.

You have completed this lesson and are ready to return to the tutorial.

25 Choose File > Exit (Windows) or File > Quit (Macintosh).

You can return to the tutorial by double-clicking the Instruct icon on the CD.

Lesson 7-2

Working with 3D Models

Note: You will need to install the training version of Extreme 3D from the CD to practice this lesson. Please read the special instructions on the first page of this section.

In this lesson, you will create three-dimensional objects from two-dimensional profiles imported from FreeHand. You will link these elements together and apply surface materials and then render a final image of the scene.

1 **Go to the Lessons folder on the CD and open the file named 7-2.e3d.**
There are no elements in this Extreme 3D document.

2 **Choose File > Import > FreeHand. Select the Fgs.fh7 document located in the Lessons folder and click Open.**
The FreeHand paths in this document are imported as four separate profiles in the workspace. (Notice that the F character consists of two pieces.)

3 **Select all four of these profiles using the Pointer tool and Shift.**
Even if these elements were grouped in FreeHand, they are imported as separate pieces. The next step is to link these four elements together.

4 **Choose the Lock Link tool from the Link tool group and click the *G* profile to link the other selected profiles to that one.**

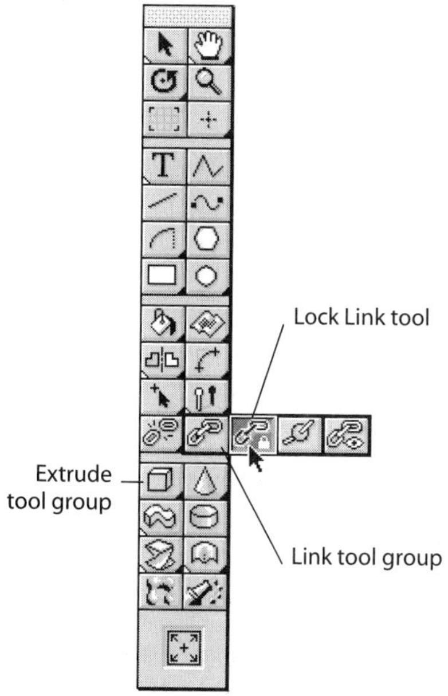

The *G* now appears in red, because it is the **parent object**. The other profiles are **child objects**, locked to the parent object. Each child object is displayed in gray.

5 **Drag any one of the profiles to center all of these linked elements on the working plane.**
The Lock Link tool locked the position of these elements in relation to one another—one element cannot be moved without the others.

Now you're ready to create three-dimensional elements based on these profiles.

6 **With the *G* still selected, choose the Bevel Extrude tool from the Extrude tool group in the toolbox.**

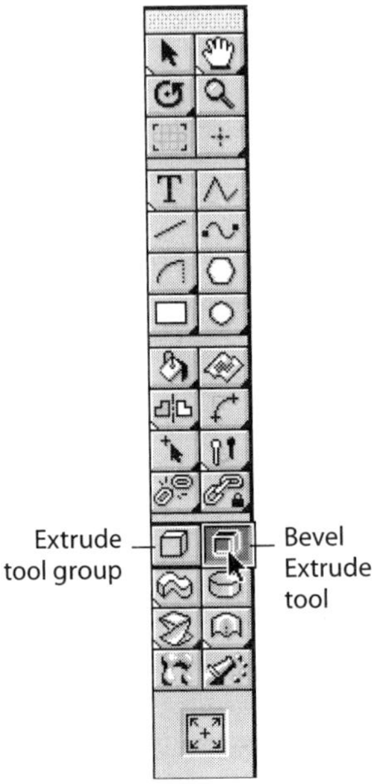

The Bevel Extrude tool creates extrusions that have rounded corners. The tool space displays the current settings for this tool; the values in the tool space are displayed in inches.

7 **In the tool space, change the extrude depth to *0.2* and the bevel width to *.02* and then press Enter (Windows) or Return (Macintosh).**

Extruding the parent profiles also extrudes the child profiles.

8 Choose View > Three-Quarters to see these 3D objects more clearly.

Now that these are three-dimensional objects, you need to reestablish the links, using the same method you originally used to link the profiles.

9 With all four pieces still selected, click the *G* with the Lock Link tool again.

10 Change back to the Front view by choosing View > Front.

Next you'll select a **material** to apply to these elements from the Materials Browser, to make this logo look more exciting.

11 Choose Window > Materials.

On the left side of this panel are the materials currently in this scene. Right now, the scene uses only the default material, Gray Plastic. On the right side of the panel is a list of other materials you can choose from.

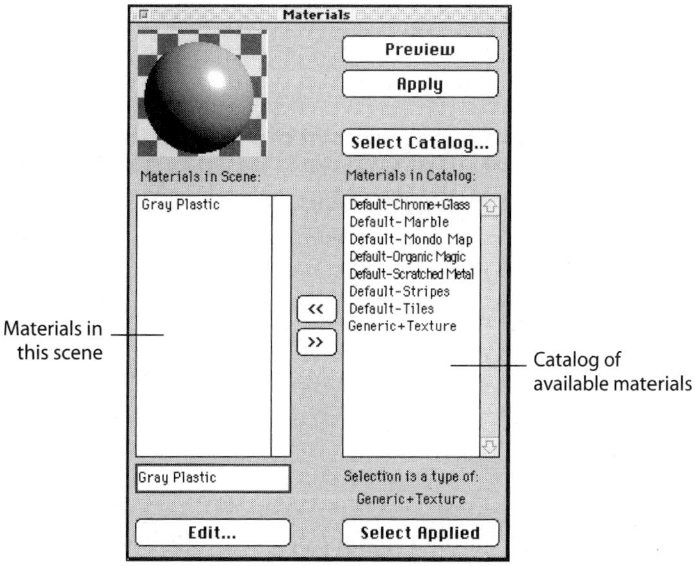

12 Double-click Default-Marble to add this material to the scene.

A new material, Default-Marble1, appears in the list on the left.

13 Double-click the marble material in the list on the left to edit this material before you apply it.

The Material Editor opens, where you can change the appearance of this material.

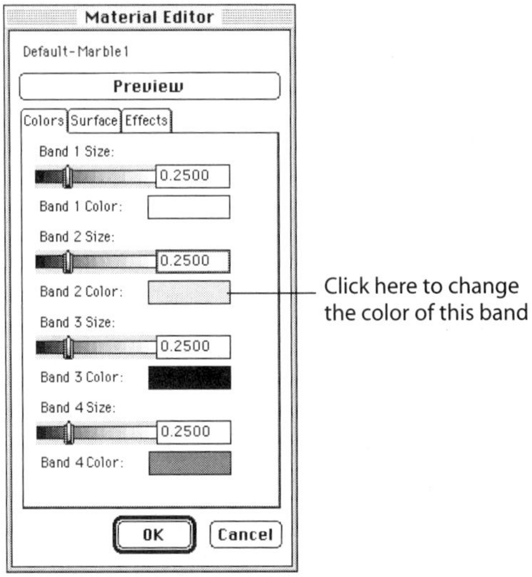

14 Change the color of one of the bands by clicking once on the color swatch, selecting a new color from the Color dialog box that appears, and clicking OK to return to the Material Editor.

The preview window at the top of the Materials Browser may not show the change in color yet.

15 Click the Preview button at the top of the Material Editor to update the preview of this material displayed at the top of the Materials Browser.

Move the Material Editor dialog box if it prevents you from seeing the preview window.

16 Click OK in the Material Editor and then click the Apply button at the top right of the Materials Browser to apply this material to the selected object.

When you apply this material, the *G* object changes color slightly to indicate a material change. However, you will not see the full detail of the material until you create a final **rendering**. Also, the material was applied only to the *G* and not to the objects linked to that element.

17 **To apply the material to all of the linked elements at once, hold down F2 (Windows) or Control (Macintosh) and click Apply in the Materials Browser.**

This applies the material down the family tree—to the parent and child objects at the same time. This is called applying a material **down-tree**.

Now you will prepare to render the final image.

18 **With the Zoom tool, drag around all the elements in the logo.**

Your view when rendering determines what you will see in the final image.

19 **Choose Render > Final Render Setup. Choose Better from the Quality menu, turn off the two Shadow options, and click OK.**

Increasing the quality setting in this dialog box improves the appearance of the final result, but it lengthens the rendering time. You can shorten rendering time when you don't need shadows to be rendered by turning off the shadow options here.

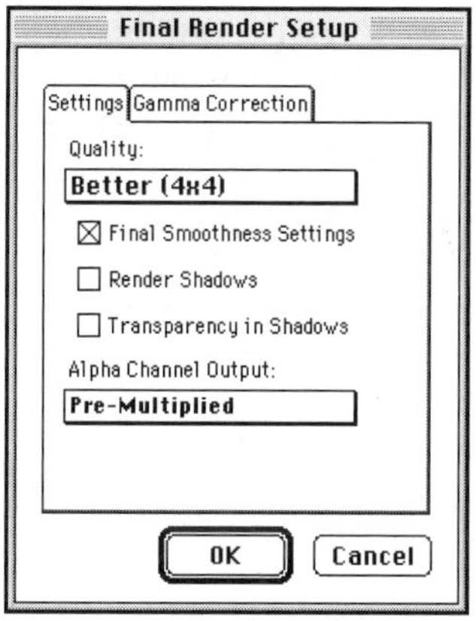

20 With all the elements still selected, choose Render > Adaptive Smoothing.

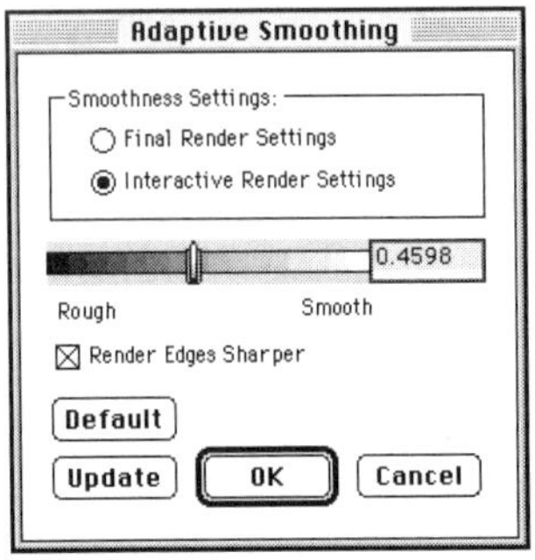

The Interactive Render settings determine how good the models look as you create and manipulate them in the workspace. Lower settings here allow you to create and manipulate models more quickly, without affecting the quality of the final rendering. However, very low settings can make circles look like polygons, with flat sides, so you need to find a balance between the quality of the screen display and the speed Extreme 3D draws the elements on the screen.

Making changes in this dialog box changes elements that are currently selected.

21 In the Adaptive Smoothing dialog box, click Final Render Settings to turn on this option.
These settings determine the smoothness of the shapes in your final output. Making these settings smoother will improve quality, but will also lengthen the rendering time for the image.

22 Drag the slider to the right slowly until the value is approximately 0.80. Then click OK.

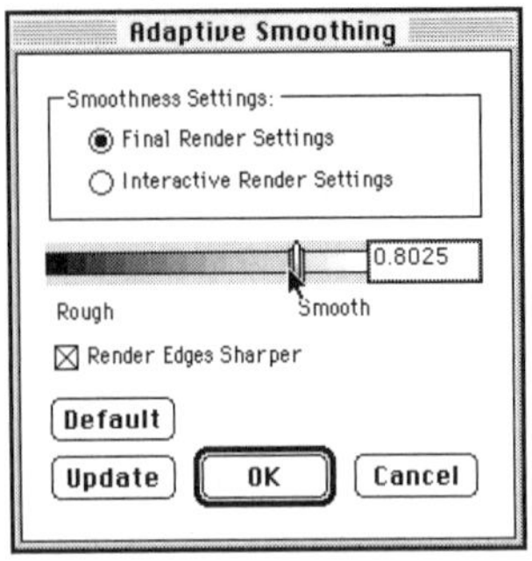

Now you are ready to render the final image.

23 Choose Render > Render to Disk.

In this dialog box, you can specify precisely how this image should be rendered. Here you will select the file format you want to use for the rendered image.

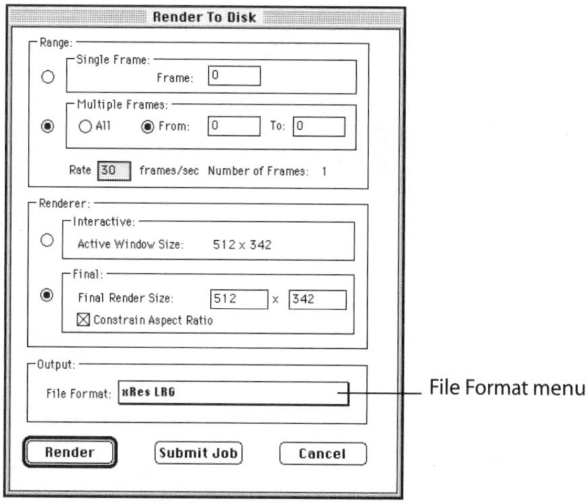

24 Select the xRes LRG format from the File Format menu at the bottom of the dialog box.

Extreme 3D can save rendered images in many of the popular print, multimedia, and Internet graphic formats. For Web graphics, this includes JPEG, GIF, and PNG formats, plus you can render animations directly to the Animated GIF format. You can also render directly to the xRes LRG format, which is useful since xRes can be used to create composite images.

25 Click the Render button. Select a location and enter a name for this image, such as *MyFgs*, in the dialog box that appears and then click Save.

26 Depending on the format you choose, an options dialog box may appear where you can control specific options your format offers. For the LRG file, choose the 32-bit with Alpha option.

This creates an image with an **alpha channel**, which records the location of the 3D elements in this scene. This alpha channel can be used in xRes as a mask to hide the white background and display only the 3D artwork. You will see how to use this alpha channel in xRes to mask out the background in Section 8 of this tutorial.

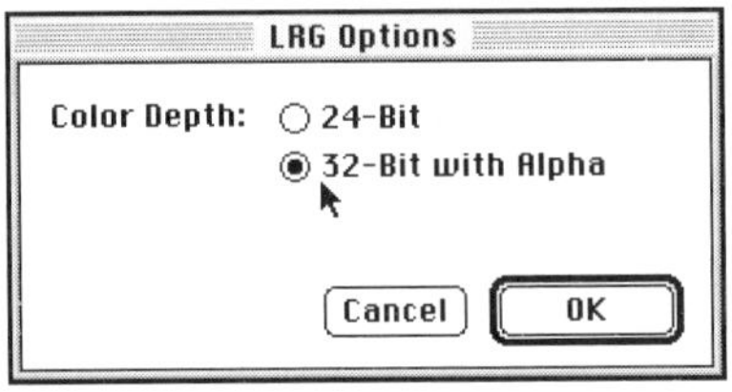

27 Click OK to render the image.

Rendering progress is displayed in the status bar at the bottom of the screen, and the final image is displayed on your screen as it is being rendered to the disk.

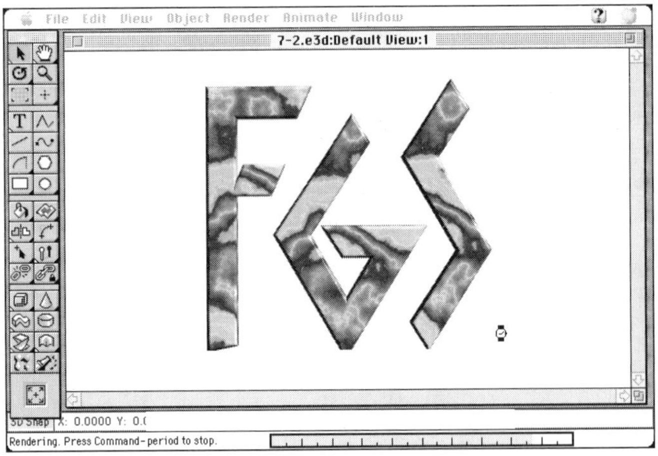

When the rendering is complete, you have completed this lesson and are ready to return to the tutorial.

28 Choose File > Exit (Windows) or File > Quit (Macintosh).

You can return to the tutorial by double-clicking the Instruct icon on the CD.

8 Adding Artistic Effects with xRes

Note: If you own a copy of xRes, you can use it to practice the lessons in this section, or you can work with the training version of xRes that is on the CD. (You do not need these programs to watch the tutorials, only to use the practice files.)

To run the training version of xRes, you need to install it on your hard drive. See the installation instructions in the introduction to this book. You will need at least 16 megabytes of RAM to run xRes (24 megabytes is recommended). If you're using a Macintosh, a Power PC is recommended; for Windows, a Pentium processor is recommended.

This section consists of two lessons:

- Getting Started with xRes
- Working with Objects and Exporting Your Artwork

Macromedia xRes, another product in the FreeHand Graphics Studio, is a powerful tool for creating, editing, and combining bitmap images. You can create digital paintings with a variety of natural, textured brushes, including charcoal, oil, and pencil. xRes also allows you to manipulate digital images and create composite digital images, with precise control over the outcome.

In this section you will create a painted texture and then combine it with other images that were created and rendered in Extreme 3D.

Lesson 8-1

Getting Started with xRes

Note: You will need to install the training version of xRes from the CD to practice this lesson. Please read the special instructions on the first page of this section.

When you launch the xRes application, you can choose to open an existing document or create a new one. In this lesson, you will start by creating a new image.

1 **Double-click the xRes application icon to launch the program.**
   No document is open at the beginning of this lesson. You will create a new document in the next step.

2 **Choose File > New.**
   The New Image dialog box appears. This is where you specify the characteristics of the image you'll be working with. Unlike FreeHand artwork, bitmap images have a fixed resolution, which you must set when you first create a document.

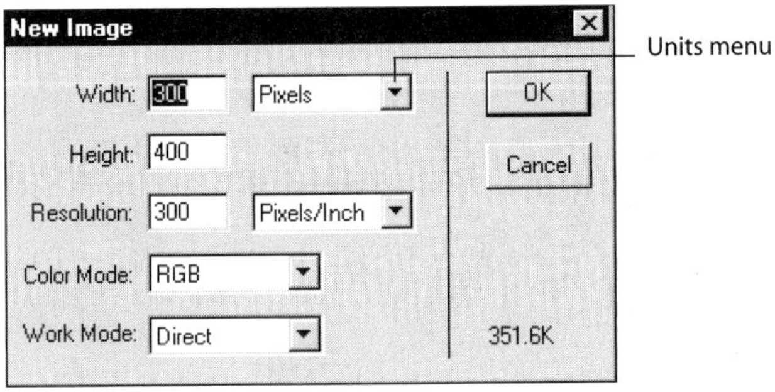

3 **Change the units to Inches and enter *4* for both the width and height. Then change the resolution to *72* pixels per inch. Make sure that Color Mode is set to RGB and Work Mode is set to Direct.**
   You can choose from two work modes when creating images. The xRes mode allows you to work quickly with very large files—for example, with files of 20 megabytes or more. (The initial size of this image is displayed in the lower-right corner of the New Image dialog box.) The Direct mode is better for smaller graphics, such as the one you'll work with here.

4 **Click OK.**

A new image window appears.

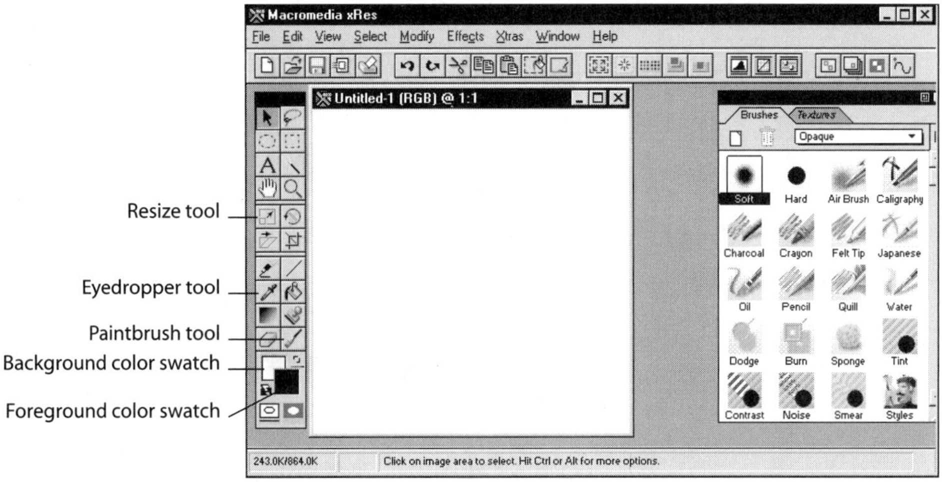

Now you will use the painting tools to create a textured background.

5 **Choose the Paintbrush tool from the toolbox and paint a stroke in the image window.**

The black, smooth stroke that appears is not what you want for this texture.

6 **Choose Edit > Undo or click the Undo button on the toolbar.**

You will need to specify how this brush should work and what color it should use before you use it to apply paint.

7 **Double-click the Foreground color swatch in the toolbox to display the Color Picker, click the pink area of the color spectrum at the bottom of the Color Picker, and select a pink color.**

Clicking anywhere in the color spectrum at the bottom of the Color Picker displays an enlarged section of that part of the spectrum at the top of the panel. You can then click the specific color desired.

Notice that your color now appears in the Foreground color swatch in the toolbox, so you can always see what color you are about to paint.

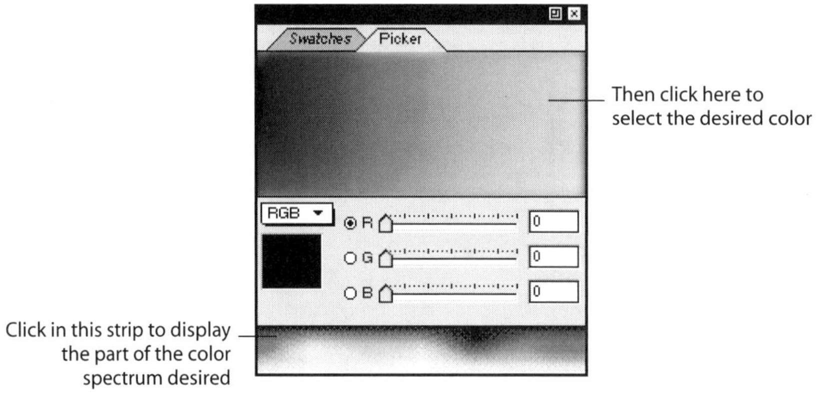

8 **Click the Airbrush in the Brushes panel at the right of the image window and then select Textured from the menu at the top of the panel.**
The paintbrush tool will now apply paint as an airbrush, using the texture selected in the Textures panel.

9 **Click the Textures tab at the top of the panel group and click to select Sandpaper as the texture for your airbrush to use.**
Now you're ready to try painting again.

10 **Paint another stroke in the image window.**
You can see the results of the changes you made, but this stroke is too thin; you need to make one more change before painting this texture.

11 **Choose Edit > Undo again. Choose Window > Inspectors > Shape and then increase the size of this brush by dragging the Size slider at the top of the Shape panel all the way to the right.**
Now the brush will cover much more area with each stroke.

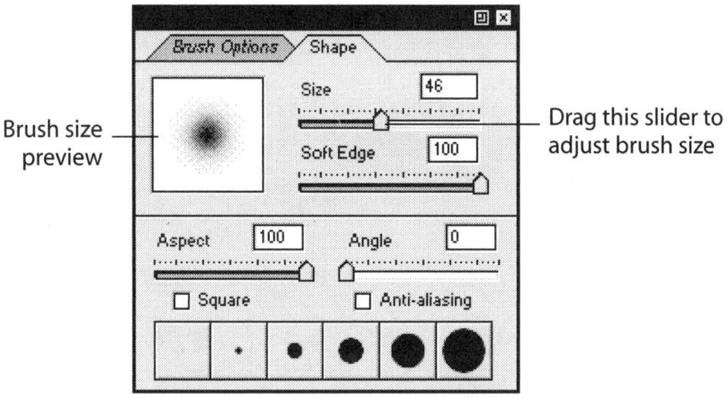

12 Drag the Paintbrush to cover the image window with the color and texture you selected.

Now you will enhance this texture by switching from the current Foreground color to a different one.

13 Double-click the Foreground color to display the Color Picker again. Click the Swatches tab at the top of this panel group and click one of the color swatches to select a new color.

The swatches panel offers an alternative to the Color Picker for selecting a color.

14 Apply more paint in the image window with this new color as you like.

As you can see, xRes gives you a great deal of control over the painting process.

You have completed this lesson and are ready to return to the tutorial.

13 Choose File > Exit (Windows) or File > Quit (Macintosh).

You can return to the tutorial by double-clicking the Instruct icon on the CD.

Lesson 8-2

Working with Objects and Exporting Your Artwork

Note: You will need to install the training version of xRes from the CD to practice this lesson. Please read the special instructions on the first page of this section.

In addition to painting tools, xRes also offers precise controls for combining images. In this lesson you will combine a painted texture with two other documents to create a finished image.

1 **Go to the Lessons folder on the CD and open the file named 8-2.mmi.**
This document contains a painted texture. To combine other images with this texture, you will use the Import command.

2 **Choose File > Import. Select the Globe.lrg file located in the Lessons folder and click Open.**
The globe, an image created and rendered in Extreme 3D, is imported along with its white background. This covers the painted texture that this document contains.

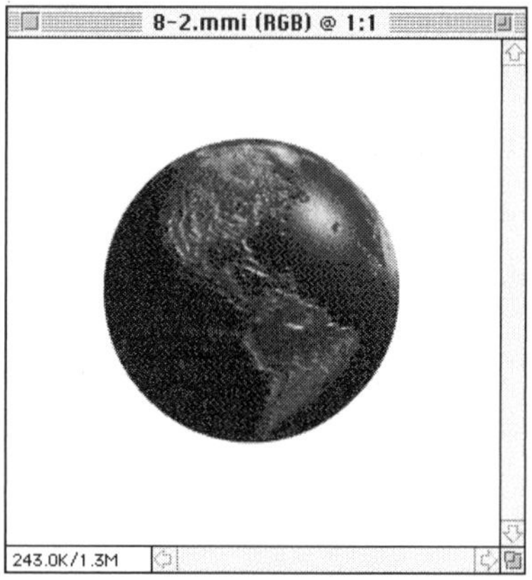

3 **Choose Window > Objects.**
As you can see, this document now contains two objects; each is a separate item that you can modify without altering the other. The globe artwork appears in front of the texture in the image because in the Objects panel the globe object is above the object that contains the texture.

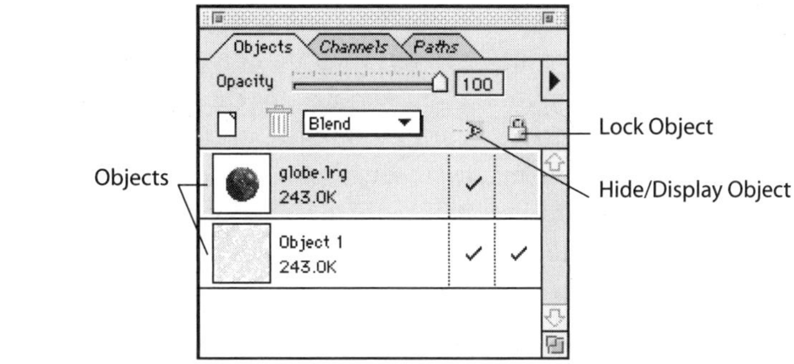

You need to hide the white area around the globe so that the painted texture shows through. First you will create a selection that contains the artwork without the white background. Then you'll store that selection and apply it to the globe object as a **mask**.

4 **Choose Window > Mask.**
The Mask panel is displayed, which enables you to identify colors that should not be included when you select the artwork. In this case, you don't want to include white.

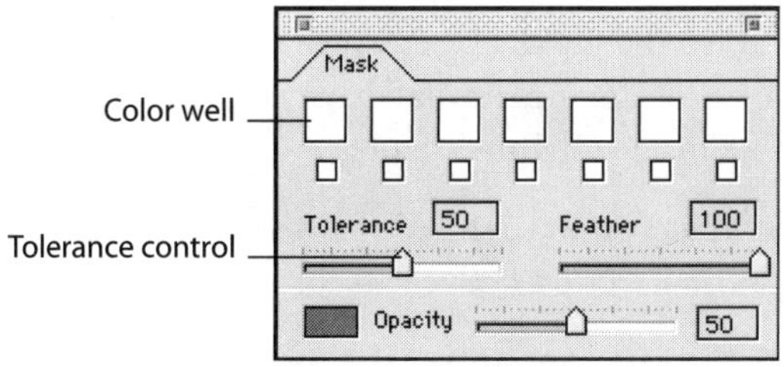

5 **Select the Eyedropper tool and click on any part of the white background in the image to select that color. Then click a color well in the Mask panel to indicate that this color should not be included in the selection.**
The Mask panel provides several color wells, which enables you to identify additional colors that should not be selected in the image, if needed. In this artwork, the globe's background is all white, so you only need to identify one color in this panel.

6 **Change the tolerance to a very low value, such as 8 or 9.**
A **tolerance** of zero will mask out only the precise color that you dropped into the Mask panel. As the tolerance value increases, the number of similar shades the mask will apply to increases.

For example, there are some very light-colored pixels inside the globe artwork, but they are not quite as bright a white as the background you sampled for the mask panel. At the original tolerance setting of 50, these near-white pixels would be included in the mask, creating holes inside the globe. By reducing the value, you reduce the number of near-white shades that will be included in the mask, and you prevent the pixels inside this globe from being affected.

7 **Choose Select > Auto to make a selection based on the settings in the Mask panel.**
All of the pixels in the object are selected except those that match the color you identified in the Mask panel (within the tolerance you set). In this case, the globe itself is selected, and the white background is not.

8 **Choose Select > Store > New to store this selection as a channel in the globe object. Then choose Select > None to deactivate the selection.**
Storing a selection enables you to recall that selection later or apply it as a mask to the object. This new selection channel is added to the globe object, since that object is active. Each object in an xRes document may have its own channels, which are visible in the Channels panel.

Now that you have stored this selection, you no longer need to have the selection active.

9 **Click the Channels tab at the top of the Objects panel group.**
The channels in this object are displayed, beginning with the red, green, and blue color channels and an RGB composite. The selection channel you stored is channel #4. (There are three color channels, so the next channel added is number 4.)

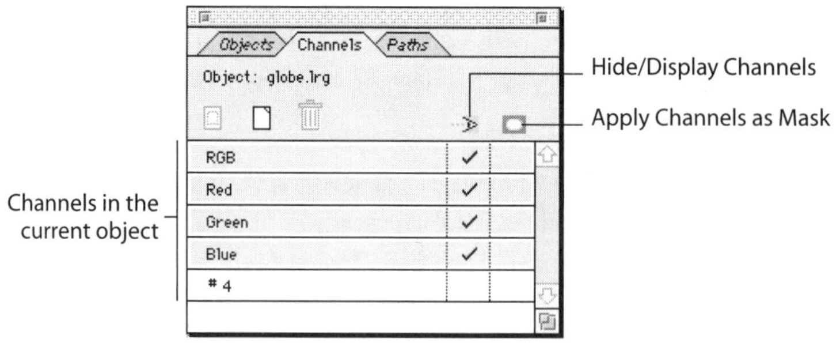

10 Click the far right column in channel #4 to apply your stored selection as a mask for this object.

A check mark appears in the column, and the white background disappears, allowing the painted texture in the object behind the globe to show through.

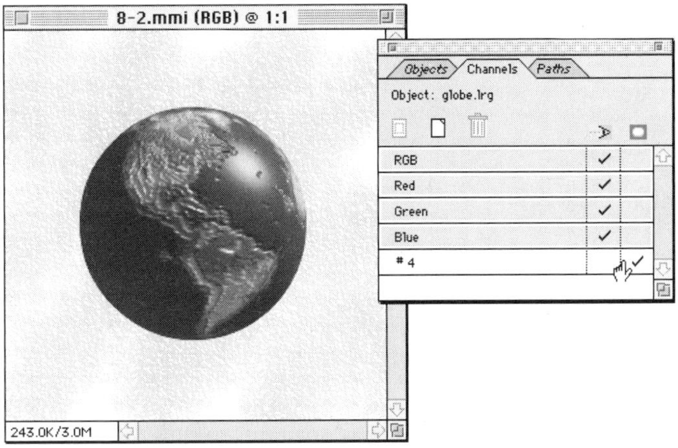

11 Click the Objects tab at the top of the panel group to display the Objects panel again.

Now you'll import another Extreme 3D image.

12 Choose File > Import. Select Fgs.lrg, located in the Lessons folder and click Open or press Enter (Windows) or Return (Macintosh).

This image is imported as another new object in the Objects panel.

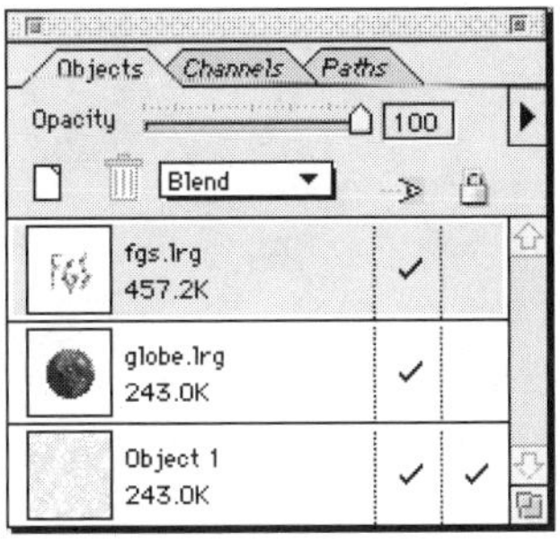

13 **Choose Modify > Align > Center to Page to center this object in the image window.**

The white background of this new object now covers the globe and texture image. Again you need to hide the white background.

14 **Display the Channels panel.**

Notice that a channel #4 already exists for this object. This is not the same channel #4 that you used for the globe object. Each object in an xRes image contains its own unique channels, and the object name is displayed at the top of the Channels panel so you know which object you are currently working with.

This image was rendered in Extreme 3D using the 32-bit with Alpha option selected. (See Section 7 in this tutorial for more information on how to create models and render images in Extreme 3D.)

Alpha in this instance refers to an **alpha channel**, which automatically saves a channel you can use to mask out the background, so only the 3D elements will appear. That alpha channel now appears in xRes as channel #4, so you can use that alpha channel in xRes to automatically hide the white background for this object.

15 **Click the far-right column for channel #4 to apply that channel as a mask for this object.**

The white background disappears, allowing you to see the artwork behind this object.

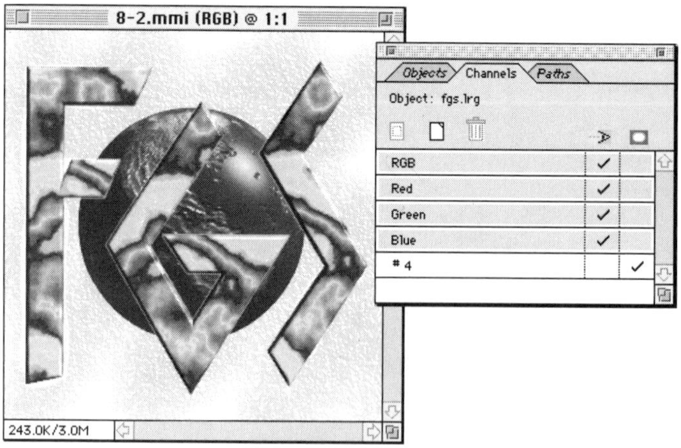

16 **To move the FGS logo behind the globe, display the Objects panel and drag the FGS object downward in the panel. Release the mouse when a heavy black line appears below the globe object.**

It is easy to reorganize the objects in your images in the Objects panel.

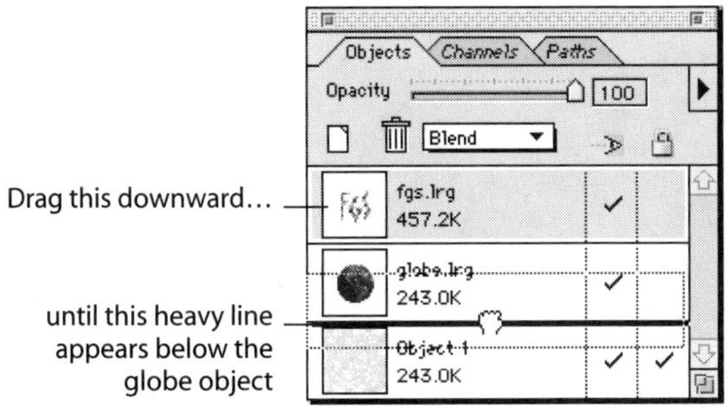

Next you will make the globe smaller and position it between the *G* and *S* characters in the logo.

17 **Click the globe object in the Objects panel.**

An object must be active for you to modify the artwork contained in that object. Only one object can be active at a time.

18 **Choose the Resize tool in the toolbox. Hold down Shift to keep the artwork in proportion and drag one of the corner selection boxes that appears around the edges of the document window to make this globe smaller.**

Only the globe artwork is resized, since that is the active object.

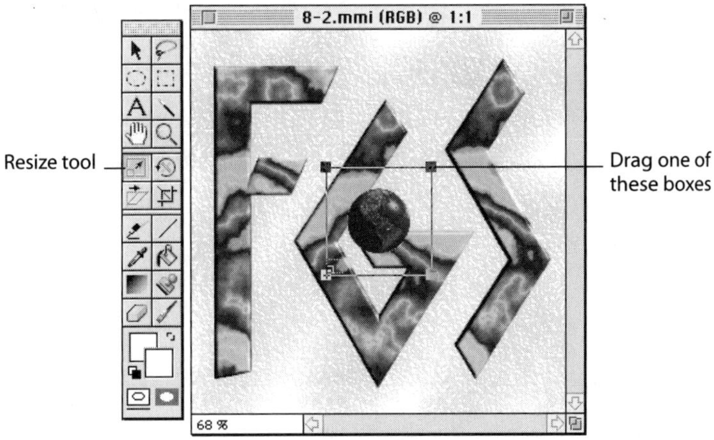

19 Use the Pointer tool to move the globe into position between the *G* and the *S* so it does not touch either character.

If it is still too large, make another adjustment using the Resize tool. When the artwork is complete, you can print from xRes or export this file for use in other applications.

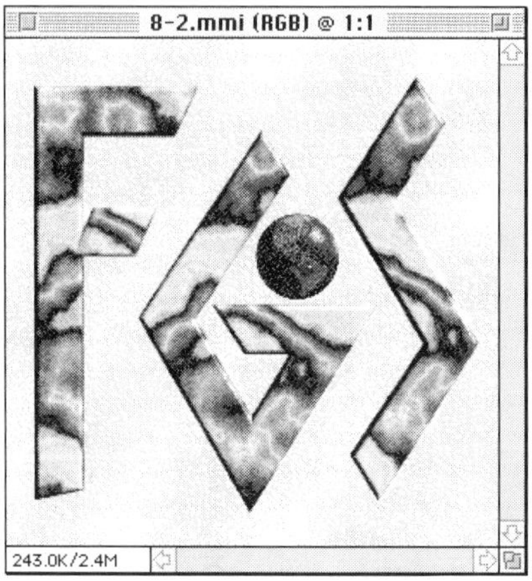

20 Choose File > Export to display a submenu containing the wide variety of bitmap graphic formats xRes exports.

In addition to many of the same bitmap image formats discussed in Section 6 of this tutorial, xRes works especially well with Adobe Photoshop—another popular image editing application. Your xRes images can be exported as Photoshop files; the objects in your image will automatically be converted to layers in Photoshop. (xRes can also open Photoshop files, which converts Photoshop layers to objects.)

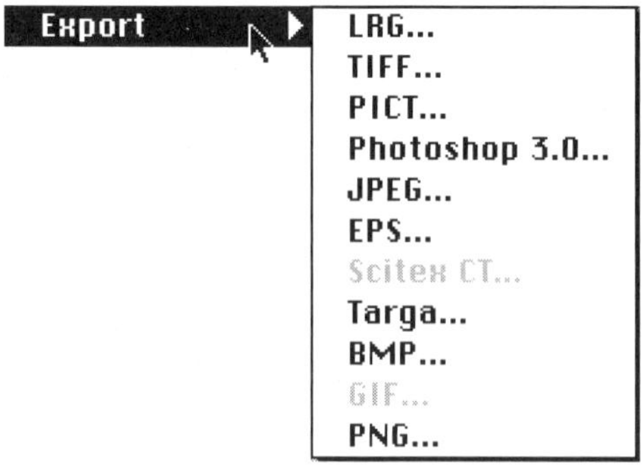

You do not need to export the image at this time. If you want, you can try exporting the artwork as a TIFF image and then importing this image into a FreeHand document to see once again how easy it is to move information between the FreeHand Graphics Studio applications.

As you can see, you can create and combine images in xRes and export them for use in your own print, multimedia, and Internet projects.

You have completed this lesson and are ready to return to the tutorial.

21 Choose File > Exit (Windows) or File > Quit (Macintosh).

You can return to the tutorial by double-clicking the Instruct icon on the CD.

9 Creating Custom Fonts with Fontographer

Note: If you own a copy of Fontographer, you can use it to practice the lessons in this section, or you can work with the training version of Fontographer that is on the CD. (You do not need these programs to watch the tutorials, only to use the practice files.)

To run the training version of Fontographer, you need to install it on your hard drive. See the installation instructions in the introduction to this book.

This section consists of two lessons:

- Creating a New Font
- Modifying an Existing Font

Macromedia Fontographer, another application in the FreeHand Graphics Studio suite, is used for creating and editing fonts. It provides tools that enable you to create new typefaces and modify existing ones for use in your print, multimedia, and Internet projects. Fontographer works with the same paths and points you use in creating FreeHand artwork and even imports EPS files you export from FreeHand. This enables you to easily create fonts containing logos, graphics, or other artwork so you can then use these elements in any of your documents by simply entering a character on the page using your custom fonts.

Lesson 9-1

Creating a New Font

Note: You will need to install the training version of Fontographer from the CD to practice this lesson. Please read the special instructions on the first page of this chapter.

In this lesson, you will create a custom font containing special characters for a logo.

1 **Double-click the Fontographer application icon to launch the program.**
No document is open at the beginning of this lesson. You will create a new document in the next step.

2 **Choose File > New Font.**
An empty **character grid** appears, where you can assign artwork for each character in the font you are creating.

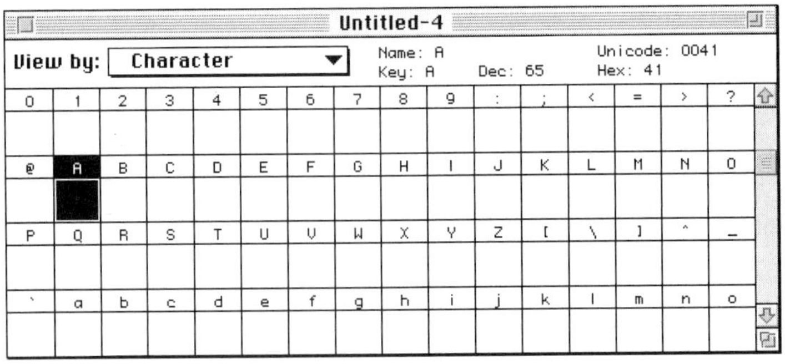

3 **Choose Element > Font Info > General (Windows) or Element > Font Info (Macintosh).**
You must enter a name for your new font in the Font Info dialog box.

4 **Enter *MyFont* as the name for this font and then click OK to return to the character grid.**
The name you enter in this dialog box is the name that will appear in the Font menu when you install the completed font.

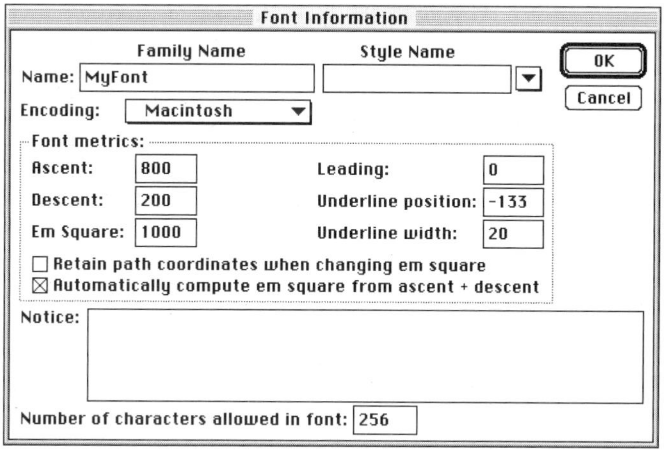

5 **Click the uppercase L in the character grid to select that character.**

One way to assign artwork to a character is to select an individual character in the grid and then import a graphic.

6 **Choose File > Import > EPS. Select the Fgs.eps file located in the Lessons folder and click Open.**

The EPS file, created in FreeHand, is imported and assigned to the selected character. After you generate and install this font, you will be able to insert this artwork into a document simply by entering an uppercase L on a page using this font.

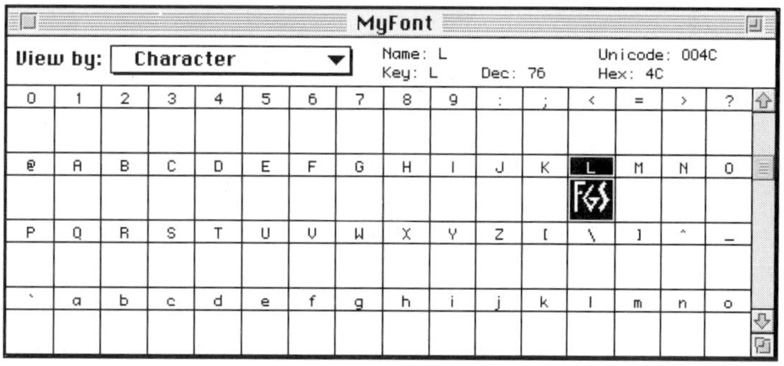

7 Double-click the artwork in the L slot of the character grid to open the outline window for this character.

The outline window displays the artwork you imported as paths. The toolbox at the left of this window is similar to FreeHand's; it contains tools you can use to modify the paths or create new ones. The two guides along the left and right sides of your character are called **sidebearings**. These indicate the normal amount of spacing around this character.

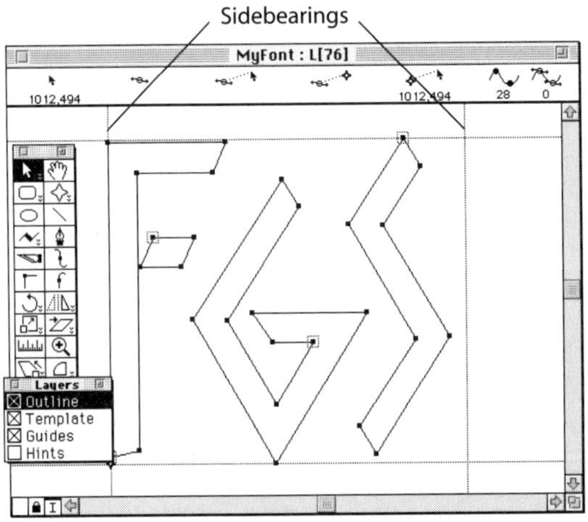

8 Choose Metrics > Equalize Sidebearings.

This command automatically balances the space on either side of the artwork. As you can see, the logo is now centered between the sidebearings.

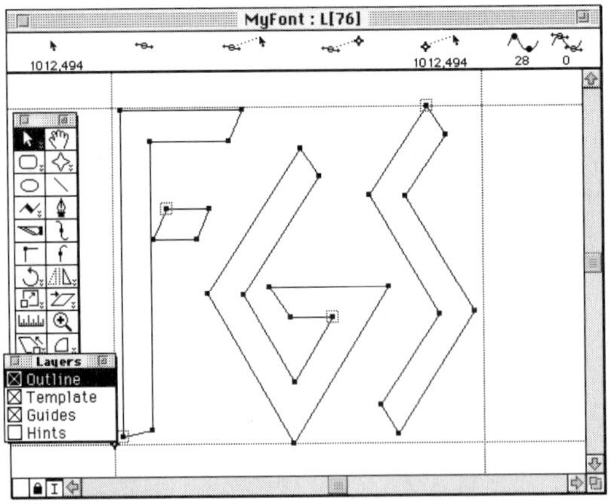

Tip: Be sure to select a different character in the character grid before importing another EPS file, to assign the new artwork to another character in the font. If you leave the same character selected, the new artwork will replace the old artwork.

9 Close the outline window to return to the character grid.

You can repeat steps 5 through 9 to assign artwork to other characters in this font. For example, the Lessons folder contains three other EPS files you can experiment with—F.eps, G.eps, and S.eps.

The next step is to generate the font.

10 Choose File > Generate Font Files and click Easy at the top of the dialog box.

Fontographer offers you a high level of control over every aspect of the characters, letterspacing, and font formats. The advanced options in this dialog box enable professional font designers to customize their font formats for specific needs.

For most needs, the Easy option is the best choice when creating fonts for general use.

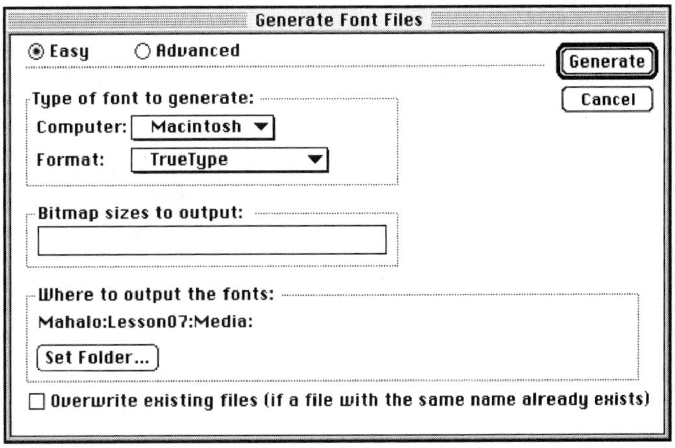

11 Select the type of computer for which you want to create this font.

Fonts can be generated for different computer systems, enabling you to use the same character artwork on different computing platforms with ease.

12 Choose TrueType as the format for the font.

Fontographer can create both TrueType and PostScript fonts.

Leave the Bitmap Sizes to Output field empty, since TrueType fonts do not require bitmaps.

13 Make sure the font will be output in the desired location. If necessary, click the Set Folder button to choose a different location.

14 Click Generate to create the font.

To use this font in your documents, you must install the font on your computer. In Windows 95, drag the font into the Fonts folder in the Control Panel. On the Macintosh, drop the font onto the System Folder's icon.

Once installed, your font is available by name in the Font menu. If you would like to see the font in action, create a new document in FreeHand and enter an uppercase L on the page. Change the font to MyFont and increase the type size so you can clearly see the results! The following illustration shows what you would see if you did this in FreeHand.

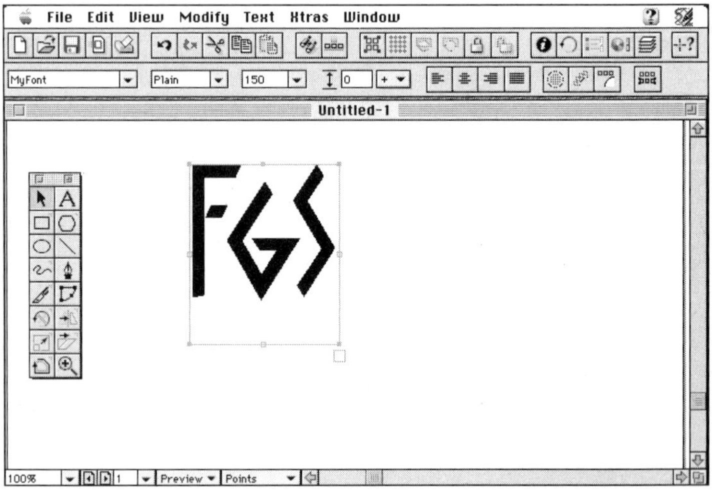

You have completed this lesson and are ready to return to the tutorial.

15 Choose File > Exit (Windows) or File > Quit (Macintosh).

You can return to the tutorial by double-clicking the Instruct icon on the CD.

Lesson 9-2

Modifying an Existing Font

Note: You will need to install the training version of Fontographer from the CD to practice this lesson. Please read the special instructions on the first page of this section.

Fontographer can also be used to modify existing fonts. For example, you can create lighter- or heavier-weight versions of a font, adjust spacing, or simply print samples of characters or keyboard layouts.

1 **Go to the Lessons folder on the CD and open the file named 9-2.fog.**
You now see the character grid for an existing TrueType font.

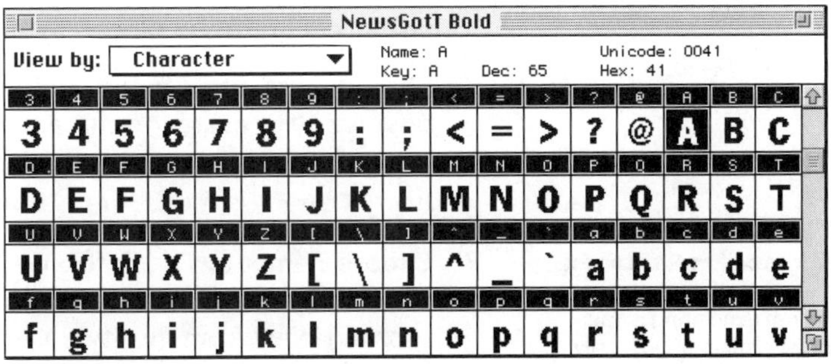

2 **Double-click the artwork in the uppercase H character slot to open the outline window for that character.**
There are many different ways to alter this artwork. In this lesson you will have Fontographer automatically change the weight of this character.

3 **Choose Element > Change Weight.**
This option enables you to easily create a heavier or lighter version of this character.

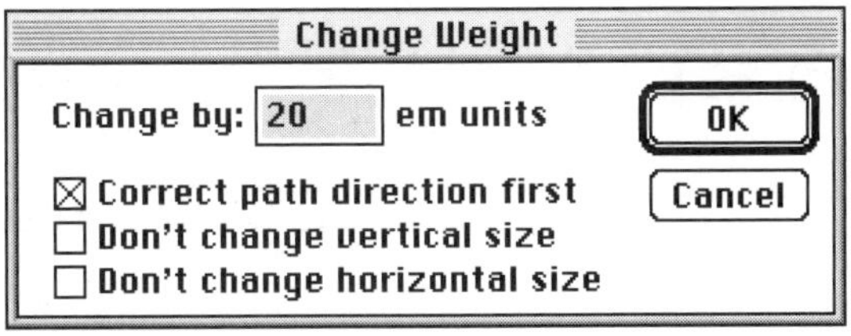

4 **To make this character thinner, enter a negative value by typing *–50*. To keep the outer dimensions of this character from changing, check the Don't change vertical size and Don't change horizontal size options. Then click OK.**

The strokes that make up this character are now thinner. In most cases, you will want to make a change like this to all of the characters in the font, so they all remain consistent with one another, so you will undo this change and apply a similar modification to the entire font.

5 **Choose Edit > Undo and close the outline window to return to the character grid.**

6 **Choose Edit > Select All to select all of the characters at once.**

Now the Change Weight command will apply to all of the characters in this font.

7 **Choose Element > Change Weight again. This time, enter positive *50* to make the characters heavier. Make sure that both Don't change options are still checked and then click OK.**

Every character in this font is now heavier than it was before.

Tip: Don't forget to change the name of this font before generating it. You don't want to accidentally replace the original font that has this name!

8 **Choose Element > Font Info > General (Windows) or Element > Font Info (Macintosh). In the dialog box, select a different weight, such as Heavy, from the Style Name menu and then click OK.**

Make sure to choose a style name that will not conflict with other versions of this font that may already exist. Notice that the weight is preceded by a hyphen in the Style Name field.

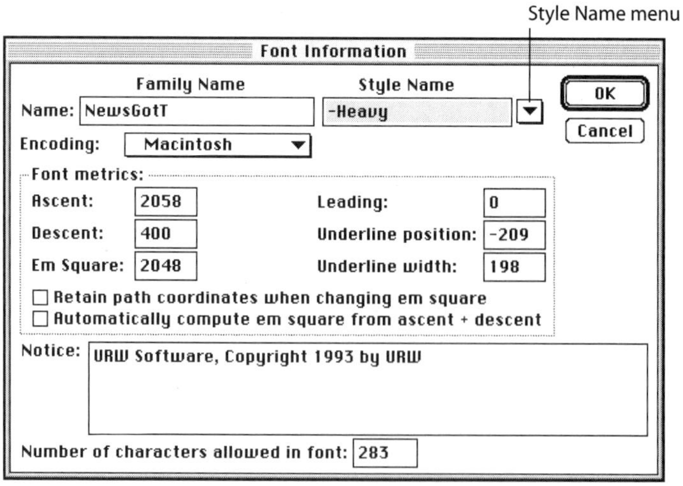

Now you are ready to generate the font.

9 **Choose File > Generate Font Files. Choose your computer platform, select TrueType as the format, and check to make sure that the font will be output in the desired location. Then click Generate.**

Now you'll have a new version of this font that is ready to be installed on your system.

You have completed this lesson and are ready to return to the tutorial.

10 **Choose File > Exit (Windows) or File > Quit (Macintosh).**

You can return to the tutorial by double-clicking the Instruct icon on the CD.

10 Creating Web Graphics with Shockwave

This section consists of two lessons:

- Preparing Graphics for the Web
- Embedding a Shocked Graphic in a Web Page

Shockwave is Macromedia technology that allows users to interact with and view dynamic media and graphics over the World Wide Web. Shockwave comes in many forms, providing tools for delivering animations, sounds, vector graphics, and high-resolution images over the Internet. Shockwave provides a high-impact way to communicate your ideas by enhancing a standard Web page with graphics that go far beyond the standard GIF and JPEG static images.

"Shocked" FreeHand graphics offer the same benefits that you enjoy while working in FreeHand, including the ability to zoom in to see artwork in greater detail.

Lesson 10-1

Preparing Graphics for the Web

Tip: The most up-to-date versions of Afterburner and the Shockwave plug-ins can always be downloaded for free from Macromedia's Web site (http://www.macromedia.com). A Shockwave developer's kit, which includes information on server configuration, tips and techniques, troubleshooting, and more, can also be downloaded from the Web site.

Note: To perform the operations in this lesson, you will not be able to use the training version of FreeHand supplied with this tutorial. You can, however, play the 10-1 tutorial and read this lesson to get a good idea of how the operation works. If you have your own copy of FreeHand 7, you can complete the exercise in this lesson.

Shockwave includes two parts: **Afterburner**, a FreeHand Xtra you will use to create Shockwave elements from your FreeHand artwork; and the free Shockwave **plug-ins**, which allow shocked elements to be incorporated and viewed on a Web page.

In this lesson, you will see how to prepare Shockwave graphics using Afterburner, so you can display FreeHand graphic files within standard HTML Web pages.

1 **If the practice lesson 10-1 isn't open, go to the Lessons folder on the CD and open the file named 10-1.fh7.**
You create artwork for use with Shockwave and the World Wide Web the same way you create any other graphic or image in FreeHand. Once your artwork is complete, you follow the steps presented here to shock it for the Web.

2 **Choose Window > Xtras > URL Editor to display a panel where you can define links to other Web pages and apply them to elements in your artwork.**
You define a link using a uniform resource locator, or URL, which is a standard address for a file or location on the Internet.

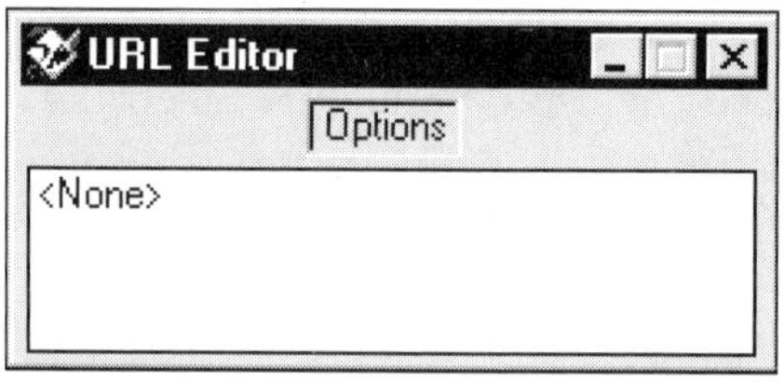

3 **Choose Options > New at the top of the URL Editor.**
A New URL dialog box appears where you can create a new address. The address of Macromedia's Web site is the default entry.

4 Enter the complete URL for the page you want to link to. In this example, click after the existing text, enter */shockwave/*, and click OK.

This is the address of a Web page where you can find more information about Shockwave.

Tip: Check the Macromedia Web site regularly to keep up with new developments in Shockwave technology.

5 Select the word *ZOO* on the page with the Pointer tool.

This is the element you want to link to the URL you just defined.

6 Click the URL you defined in the URL Editor panel to assign the URL and make the selected element a link.

There is no limit to the number of URLs or links you can assign in a single Shockwave graphic.

You can easily check to see if links have already been assigned to elements. Simply select an object on the page, and if a URL is selected in the URL Editor, that URL is assigned to this element. If no URL is selected, then no URL has been assigned.

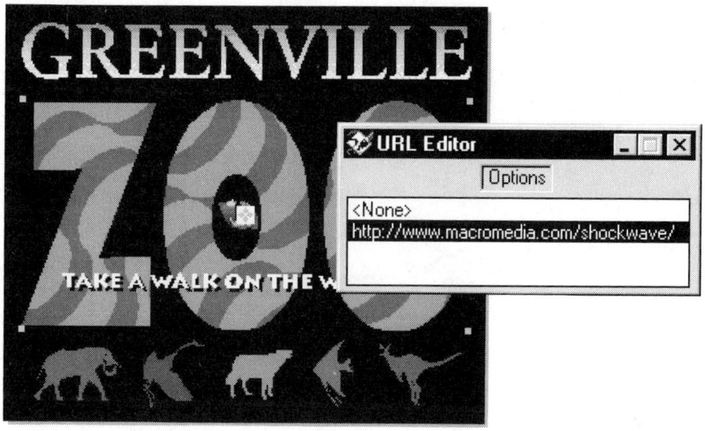

Next you must adjust the page size to match the size of the graphic and identify the size of the page in points. In this example, the page size is already set to match the graphic, so no changes will be required.

7 **Display the Document Inspector by choosing Window > Inspectors > Document. Change the measurement units for this document to points using the Measurement Units menu at the bottom of the screen. Make a note of the width and height of the page so you can use those values later.**
When your graphic is embedded in a Web page, you will need to enter the width and height of the page in pixels, using the same values as those displayed here in points.

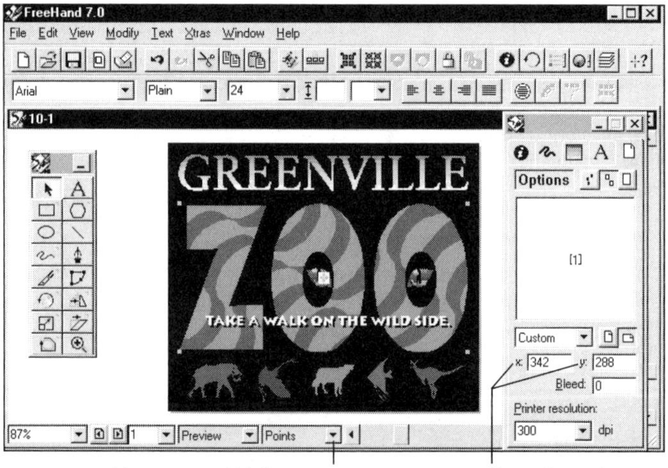

Measurement Units menu
Page dimensions

8 **Save the changes in the document.**
Now you're ready to compress this file for the Web.

9 **Choose Xtras > Afterburner > Compress Document.**
A dialog box appears where you can choose a location, name, and options for a compressed version of this artwork.

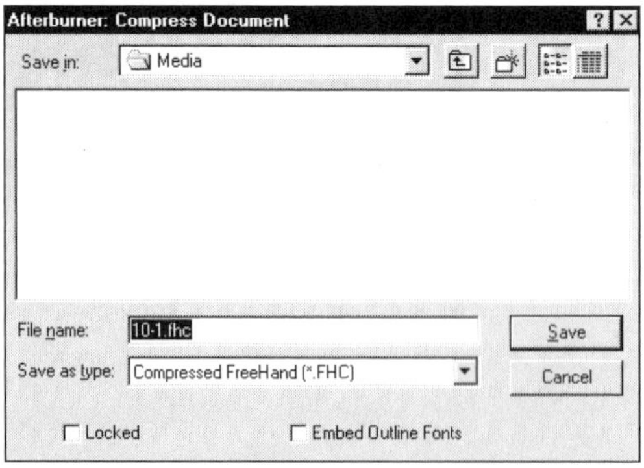

Afterburner is a compression tool that reduces the size of a graphic without changing its quality. This will allow the artwork to be downloaded more quickly for viewing on the Web. Afterburner saves a version of your graphic in the FreeHand Compressed, or FHC, format. A compressed file must have the .fhc extension at the end of its name for the Web browser to properly display the graphic.

Locked files cannot be decompressed later, so if you don't want others to be able to download and open your graphic, turn on the Locked option here. If your graphic contains PostScript Type 1 or TrueType fonts, including fonts you create in Fontographer, you can embed the character shapes in the Shockwave graphic.

In this document, all of the text has already been converted to paths so a gradient fill and other special effects could be applied, so you don't need to embed outline fonts for this graphic.

10 Click Save to compress the file.

A message will confirm that the file was compressed successfully.

The Afterburner compression reduces the size of the graphic considerably. For this document, Afterburner reduced the file size from approximately 61 kilobytes for the FreeHand document to about 24 kilobytes for the FHC file.

You have completed this lesson and are ready to return to the tutorial.

11 Choose File > Exit (Windows) or File > Quit (Macintosh).

If you opened this lesson file from within the interactive tutorial, you will be returned to the tutorial automatically. Otherwise, you can return to the tutorial by double-clicking the Instruct icon on the CD.

Lesson 10-2

Embedding a Shocked Graphic in a Web Page

Note: In this lesson, you will need a Web browser that supports Shockwave, along with the Shockwave for FreeHand plug-in for your browser. The plug-in is available on the CD or can be downloaded from Macromedia's Web site.

If you do not have these tools, you can still gain valuable information by playing the 10-2 tutorial and reading this lesson. You will learn how to write the code that places a Shockwave graphic on a Web page.

In this lesson you will see how to place your Shockwave graphic on a Web page using the Embed command. Then you will see Shockwave in action, by exploring your Shocked FreeHand graphic in a Web browser.

There are two ways to complete the first step in this lesson, since you will be viewing—but not making changes to—the code that embeds the Shockwave graphic in a Web page. Either open the document in a text editor to view it on your screen or look at the following illustration, which shows the same view of the document.

1 **Look at the following illustration or open the Zoo.htm document in a text editing application, such as WordPad (Windows) or SimpleText (Macintosh). This document is located in the Lessons folder on the CD.**
   This is what a Web page looks like in a word processor. Web pages are written in hypertext markup language, or **HTML.**

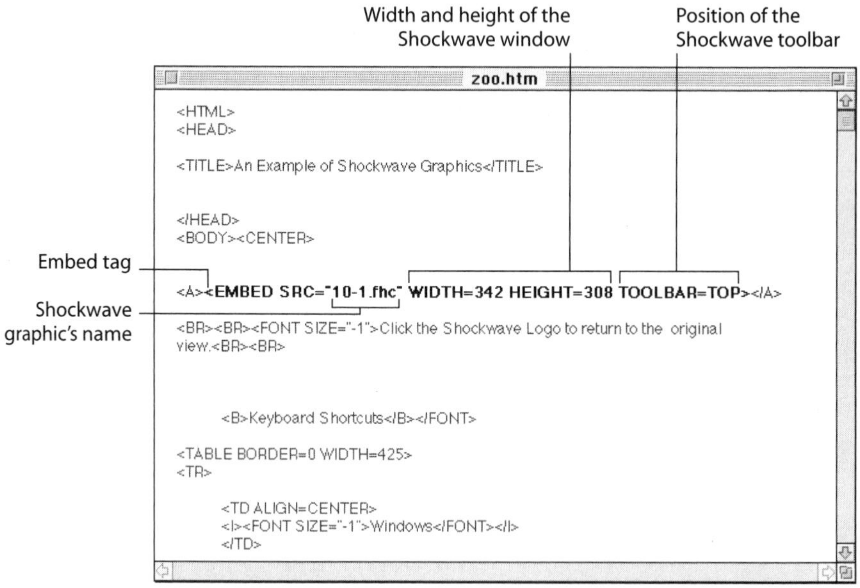


```
<HTML>
<HEAD>

<TITLE>An Example of Shockwave Graphics</TITLE>


</HEAD>
<BODY><CENTER>

<A><EMBED SRC="10-1.fhc" WIDTH=342 HEIGHT=308 TOOLBAR=TOP></A>

<BR><BR><FONT SIZE="-1">Click the Shockwave Logo to return to the original
view.<BR><BR>


        <B>Keyboard Shortcuts</B></FONT>

<TABLE BORDER=0 WIDTH=425>
<TR>

        <TD ALIGN=CENTER>
        <I><FONT SIZE="-1">Windows</FONT></I>
        </TD>
```

Notice the Embed command, or **tag**, used to incorporate the FreeHand graphic into this page. HTML tags are enclosed in angle brackets (< >). Embed begins by identifying the source file—the name of the graphic. Then the width and height are indicated in pixels, using the page size values measured in points in FreeHand. The last instruction identifies the position of the **Shockwave toolbar**. The toolbar can be attached to the top or bottom of a Shockwave element; if you omit this instruction from the Embed command, your graphic will be displayed without a toolbar. If you do include a toolbar, you must add 20 pixels to the height of your document, as was done here, to make room for this element.

If you opened the document in a text editor, you can choose File > Exit (Windows) or File > Quit (Macintosh) now.

2 **Drag the Zoo.htm document located in the Lessons folder and drop it on the icon for your Web browser.**
This launches the browser and opens the Web page containing the shocked graphic. The artwork appears on this Web page, looking just as it does in FreeHand.

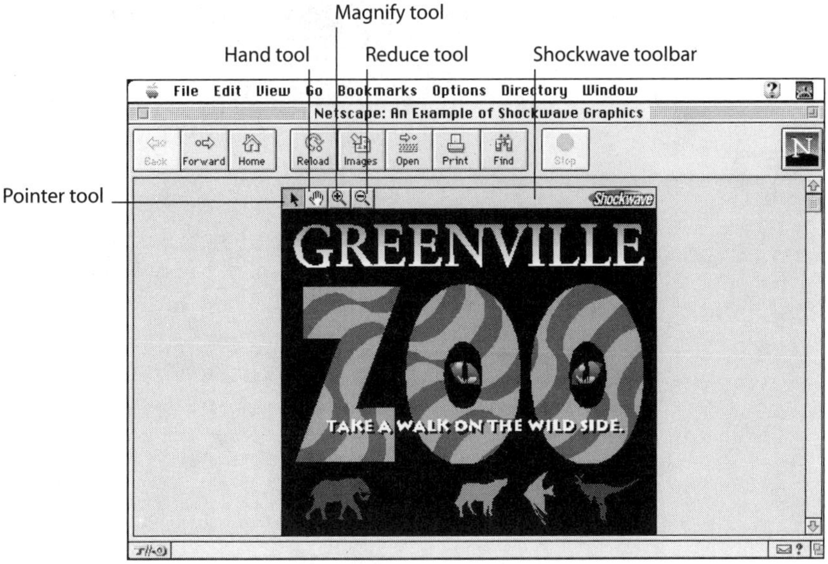

The tools available in the toolbar enable you to zoom in, pan to see other portions of the artwork, and zoom out. You use the Pointer tool to click a link in the graphic.

3 **Move the cursor over the artwork and notice that the pointer changes to a pointing hand to indicate an element that is linked to other locations on the Internet.**

These are the elements that were assigned URLs in FreeHand. When you are connected to the Internet, clicking these linked elements immediately takes you to a different page.

Hand cursor indicates that this element contains a link

4 **Zoom in on any part of the artwork by clicking with the Magnify tool or dragging to surround an area, just as you would in FreeHand.**

The artwork displays the same degree of detail and sharpness that you expect from FreeHand graphics. This is very different from GIF or JPEG files, the two graphic formats commonly used for Web pages. These formats always display graphics at a fixed size and resolution.

5 **Hold down Control and Shift (Windows) or Command and Shift (Macintosh) and click the artwork to return to the original view.**
As you can see, Shockwave technology makes it easy to incorporate FreeHand artwork into your own Web pages.

You have completed this lesson and are ready to return to the tutorial.

6 **Choose File > Exit (Windows) or File > Quit (Macintosh).**
If you opened this lesson file from within the interactive tutorial, you will be returned to the tutorial automatically. Otherwise, you can return to the tutorial by double-clicking the Instruct icon on the CD.

We hope you've enjoyed your experience with *FreeHand Graphics Studio Interactive*. Remember that you can refer to this tutorial as often as you wish. If you would like to continue your FreeHand training, visit the Macromedia Web site and look for other titles from Macromedia Press.

Now go practice the techniques you have learned and create your own designs, layouts, and illustrations!

Index

C

D

E

G

H

I

K

L

M

N

O

P

Q

R

S

U

V

W

X

Z

Macromedia tech support number: 415-252-9080